Branding in Governance and Public Management

Routledge Critical Studies in Public Management

EDITED BY STEPHEN P. OSBORNE

The study and practice of public management has undergone profound changes across the world. Over the last quarter century, we have seen

- increasing criticism of public administration as the over-arching framework for the provision of public services,
- the rise (and critical appraisal) of the 'New Public Management' as an emergent paradigm for the provision of public services,
- the transformation of the 'public sector' into the cross-sectoral provision of public services, and
- the growth of the governance of inter-organizational relationships as an essential element in the provision of public services

In reality these trends have not so much replaced each other as elided or co-existed together—the public policy process has not gone away as a legitimate topic of study, intra-organizational management continues to be essential to the efficient provision of public services, whist the governance of inter-organizational and inter-sectoral relationships is now essential to the effective provision of these services.

Further, whilst the study of public management has been enriched by contribution of a range of insights from the 'mainstream' management literature it has also contributed to this literature in such areas as networks and inter-organizational collaboration, innovation and stakeholder theory.

This series is dedicated to presenting and critiquing this important body of theory and empirical study. It will publish books that both explore and evaluate the emergent and developing nature of public administration, management and governance (in theory and practice) and examine the relationship with and contribution to the over-arching disciplines of management and organizational sociology.

Books in the series will be of interest to academics and researchers in this field, students undertaking advanced studies of it as part of their undergraduate or postgraduate degree and reflective policy makers and practitioners.

Branding in Governance and Public Management

Jasper Eshuis and Erik-Hans Klijn

Routledge
Taylor & Francis Group

NEW YORK LONDON

First published 2012
by Routledge
711 Third Avenue, New York, NY 10017

Simultaneously published in the UK
by Routledge
2 Park Square, Milton Park, Abingdon, Oxon OX14 4RN

*Routledge is an imprint of the Taylor & Francis Group,
an informa business*

First issued in paperback 2012

Typeset in Sabon by IBT Global.

Library of Congress Cataloging-in-Publication Data
Eshuis, Jasper, 1972–
    Branding in governance and public management / by Jasper Eshuis and
Erik-Hans Klijn.
        p. cm. — (Routledge critical studies in public management ; 8)
Includes bibliographical references and index.
    1. Communication in public administration.   2. Public relations and
politics.   3. Government publicity.   4. Branding (Marketing)   I. Klijn,
Erik-Hans.   II. Title.
    JF1525.C59E75 2011
    352.7'48—dc23
    2011026118

ISBN13: 978-0-415-88517-1 (hbk)
ISBN13: 978-0-203-14515-9 (ebk)
ISBN13: 978-0-415-81791-2 (pbk)

Contents

Figures

Tables

1 The Rise of Branding in Governance Processes

1.1 THE RISE OF BRANDING IN GOVERNANCE PROCESSES

In July 2007 the Dutch minister Ella Vogelaar launches a policy plan on urban renewal called Action Plan Power Communities (VROM 2007). The aim of the policy is to improve the situation in 40 Dutch communities where the quality of the living environment lags behind other Dutch communities due to an accumulation of social and economic problems. With this plan, the minister follows up on the coalition agreement, which used the term "problem communities." In the policy plan, the ministry explains that the name has been changed from problem communities to "power communities" for two reasons: firstly because the term problem community insufficiently reflects the positive aspects of the communities, and secondly because the people in the communities think that the term problem community does not reflect their perception of the community (VROM 2007). From then on, the ministry's urban renewal policies acquire a clear name: the power community policy. By introducing the distinguishing term power communities and associating the policies with positivity, power, and belief in the people, the ministry brands its policies on urban communities. By taking into account the perception of the communities, both the policies and the minister are positioned as responsive and empathic. It is noteworthy that the policies are branded not only in terms of their content, but also in terms of the process. The ministry stresses repeatedly that the policy plan is the result of a process in which the minister visited the communities to listen to their ideas.

Notwithstanding all the efforts, the implementation of the policies proves very difficult. A major reason is that the minister has few financial resources. Her resultant dependency on housing associations gradually weakens her position. In addition, the minister's media performance is widely criticized. She enlists the services of a spin doctor to improve her image, but this does not reduce the criticism. It even turns against her when the spin doctor comments negatively on her in the media (Van Kemenade 2008). When questioned about the spin doctor by a journalist, the minister gives a bad impression by failing to give an answer at all[1] (NRC 2008).

Her weak media performance becomes even more problematic when her own political party, the Social Democrats, starts to feel that the minister is weakening the party's brand. The party finally concludes that the minister has lost her authority (e.g. De Pers 2008). The problems in the governance process combined with her negative media performances eventually lead to the minister's forced resignation in November 2008 (see e.g. Van Kemenade 2008; Trouw 2008).

The Rise of Governance . . . and Branding

The example of this Dutch policy on urban renewal illustrates the usage of branding in governance processes. It shows how a policy is branded, among other things by giving it a clear and distinguishable name and associating it with feelings of positivity, empathy, and responsiveness. The name, which is the discursive and most concrete manifestation of the symbolic brand, is important to identify the policy and distinguish it from other policies. The example also indicates that, although branding may effectively influence perceptions about a policy or a politician for a while, it is not a silver bullet that can completely prevent the development of negative perceptions. Finally, the example illustrates how governance processes take place in a mediatized world. Media interventions can enhance dynamics and cause a sudden acceleration of governance processes when the full lights of the media undermine managers' positions or force them to act. As elaborated further in this book, politicians and managers try to create brands for policy objects, policy processes, and themselves to manage perceptions, activate and bind actors, and maintain their authority in mediatized governance processes.

The worldwide governance landscape in which branding takes place is characterized by governments applying new forms of horizontal governance, such as public–private partnerships (PPPs) (S. P. Osborne 2000; Hodge and Greve 2005), interactive decision making, stakeholder involvement (McLaverty 2002; Edelenbos and Klijn 2006), and other forms of citizen involvement (Lowndes et al. 2001). Many reasons have been offered to explain this phenomenon, the most common one being that the role of governments is changing. Governments in recent years have become more dependent on societal actors to achieve their goals because of the increasing complexity of the challenges they face. Many of these challenges involve conflicting values, and addressing them demands governments that are multifaceted and increasingly horizontal (Kickert et al. 1997; Sørenson and Torfing 2007).

The upsurge of *governance* means that various actors are included in policymaking and implementation processes. Private actors, social alignments, and citizens each have important resources and the power to obstruct policy interventions, but they also have different perceptions and interests. This is the governance context in which branding has become one of the strategies that politicians and public managers use to manage perceptions, but also to bind actors and to cope with media attention.

Branding as an Empirical Phenomenon

Although branding has not been applied as widely in governance processes as it has been in the private sector, political leaders and public managers do undertake a multitude of attempts to cast new brands in order to influence public opinion and stakeholder perceptions. Brands, being symbolic constructs that add value or meaning to something in order to distinguish it from its competitors, are increasingly used in strategies for managing perceptions in the public sector. Branding has been used to influence public perceptions of persons, places, organizations, projects, and physical objects such as transport infrastructure and buildings (see e.g. Eshuis and Edelenbos 2009; Evans 2003; Pasotti 2010). In particular, political branding and city branding are applied rather widely.

Political branding is applied to political leaders, political parties, policies, and coalitions. American politicians have been using marketing techniques, such as branding, public polling, and costumer segmentation, for almost five decades (Shama 1976). Former U.S. president George W. Bush used branding extensively, as the current president Barack Obama does today, to enhance their popularity, create an image, and evoke emotions with the voters. George W. Bush branded himself as a straightforward man and a strong leader. During his electoral campaign, Barack Obama branded himself as the charismatic leader who would bring change and give new hope to America. Among other brand elements, he used a logo based on the letter "O" that was carefully designed to include the colors blue and red (symbolizing that this election was not about red states versus blue states, but about a single united America). Within the logo there is a soft white glow that suggests sunrise, and symbolizes the dawn of a new day (Wheeler 2009, 254–55).

Branding techniques are now common practice among European politicians as well. Some famous proponents include Silvio Berlusconi and

Figure 1.1 The logo used by Barack Obama during his presidential campaign.

Figure 1.2   Brand elements used by German Chancellor Angela Merkel and British Prime Minister David Cameron.

Nicholas Sarkozy, as well as Angela Merkel and David Cameron. They have used branding, including brand elements such as slogans, wordmarks, and logos (see Figure 1.2), to construct an identity that is attractive to voters. In Great Britain, political parties extensively brand their parties and leaders (Harris and Lock 2001; Lees-Marshment 2001; Taylor 2007).

Tony Blair's "New Labour" and associated brand the "Third Way" is an example of branding that refers to both new policy content and a policy style. In terms of content, the Third Way refers to a position between the traditional Labour themes of improving public services and fighting social inequalities, and Thatcher's Conservative policies of privatization, lower taxes, and labor flexibility. The Third Way brand sets Blair apart from former leaders of both the Conservative Party and the Labour Party. In marketing terms, the brand differentiates Blair and his policies from competitors. The policy style stresses being with the people, instead of above the people. The Third Way brand selects certain problems and solutions and sets them out as being important. It argues that the political problem is not a surfeit of government but rather a lack of organization, and that government would function well if it partnered with societal organizations. Years after the Third Way was introduced, it was expanded by adding ideas like "joined-up government" and "partnerships." Thus, the basic idea of the Third Way was elaborated and new ideas were introduced into the political market by using the original brand. This is an example of how a brand can be leveraged by adding new concepts and ideas to it (brand extension) (Loken et al. 2010). Brand extensions are often used to reach new audiences or revitalize existing brands at a relatively low cost. After all, an existing brand that has already proved its value is being built upon.

Branding has also become common in place branding or city branding. *Branding places* focuses on geographical locations, such as nations, cities, regions, and communities. Brands communicate selected physical and emotional attributes of a place, thus giving it specific meaning. Place branding is aimed at attracting residents, tourists, or investors. It is not only major cities such as Glasgow (*Glasgow: Scotland with style*), New York (*I love New York*), Amsterdam, and Hong Kong (*Asia's world city*) that have launched branding campaigns to position themselves in the minds of citizens and tourists, but also smaller cities such as Dundee in Scotland, Nyköping in Sweden, or Randers in Denmark (see Smidt-Jensen 2005), although it has been extremely difficult to empirically establish the extent to which branding has been effective in realizing those aims (see Chapter 7). Even in the case of campaigns that are generally seen as successful, for example the *I love New York* campaign, the question of effectiveness is hard to answer. Parties involved in the campaign have emphasized that awareness of the city of New York has gone up, and that perceptions about the city have become more positive, since the start of the campaign (Greenberg 2008). They point at correlations between the campaign and changing perceptions. They do acknowledge, though, that a causal relationship between the campaign and improvements in tourism cannot be proved (Greenberg 2008, 214–17).

Until now, the use of brands and branding in governance processes has been most common in the political part of governance processes, and in the governance of cities. But the examples of the Dutch revitalization policy and of the Third Way show that politicians and managers have also started to use brands to brand policies and policy programs in governance processes. In the examples, branding was used both to highlight and distinguish the content of the policy and to communicate favorable aspects of the policy process. And we see more and more governance processes that make use of branding or elements of it to create images of content, processes, or actors in these processes. In many cases, the branding of governance processes is still in its infancy in the sense that the positioning of the governance process relies heavily on text and rational discourse, and less on the (visual) type of symbols and emotions on which private brands are built. Also, the focus is often on sending messages. For example, governance process websites are mostly relatively static and non-interactive compared to many private websites. Although the interactive and citizen-based possibilities of brands are not used to the full, branding definitely has its place in governance processes, as will be seen in the examples provided throughout this book.

Aim of This Book: Explore the Relation between Branding and Governance

Brands have become empirical phenomena in governance, but their application has received relatively little attention in public administration and policy sciences. In this book, we explore the use of brands and branding in governance processes, arguing that brands are used for a reason in such processes. Brands fit the mediatized world in which governance processes increasingly take place. By branding, public managers seek alternative ways to influence people's ideas about policy content and policy processes, but they also use branding to motivate people and attract them to governance processes. In this first chapter, we explore the relation between governance and branding and set the stage for the rest of the book.

In section 1.2, we start with a short exploration of brands as phenomena: what are they and where do we see them in governance processes? In section 1.3, we discuss the other core concept of this book—governance—and explain how we define governance and where we stand in the governance discussion. Section 1.4 argues why branding has arisen in contemporary governance processes. We argue that this is related to particular characteristics of governance processes such as the need to charm and appeal to actors on whom one depends. We also relate branding to the rise of the media society.

1.2   BRANDS AS MEANINGFUL IMAGES IN GOVERNANCE PROCESSES

One of the interesting things about branding is that it brings new strategies into the field of governance, and new questions that need to be answered as well. Branding differs from the rational and deliberative forms of communication that have dominated governance processes so far, because it is largely based on visual images and communicating emotions. Blair's brands New Labour and the Third Way appealed to citizens because they felt connected to a new movement that wanted to renew the state and society. It felt like a new and fresh force. New Labour was able to empathize with more than the traditional core voters and reach out emotionally to a wide audience by envisioning a caring, sharing state in which there would also be ample room for private initiatives and empowerment of individuals through communities. New Labour successfully countered emotions of fear that the Labour government would ally too closely with the unions and again cause deep conflicts with employers as Great Britain had experienced under Labour at the end of the 1970s. The example of New Labour and the Third Way illustrate how brands create associations with emotions. In this section, we further explain the working of brands. We explain what brands are and through what characteristics they work in governance processes. Chapter 2 deals in more depth with what brands are.

Brands: What Are They?

A brand is a symbolic construct that consists of a name, term, sign, symbol, or design, or a combination of these, intended to identify a phenomenon and differentiate it from similar phenomena by adding particular meaning to it. A brand is not the product itself; it is what gives meaning and value to the product and defines its identity (Kapferer 1992). Branding is an approach within marketing that aims at increasing the value to a user of a branded object, such as a place, by giving the object symbolic meaning that is valuable in the psychological and social life of consumers (Arvidsson 2006; Danesi 2006). Someone who buys a BMW car is buying not only a vehicle for transport, but also identity and social status. A brand is thus a sign that evokes the associations through which an object is imbued with cultural meaning (cf. Danesi 2006). For example, the BMW brand evokes such associations as "safety," "success," and "high achievement." These associations make the car valuable to the consumer both psychologically (i.e. it offers safety) and socially (i.e. it offers social status).

A brand suggests a particular experience of a product (Arvidsson 2006). For example, the negative brands that some public organizations have as being bureaucratic influence how their policies are experienced by the public, even before their policies have been implemented. People may associate a public bureaucracy with a lack of action and lack of attention to individuals' needs. Although research shows that in some countries the image of the public bureaucracies is actually quite good and better than that of politicians (Sociaal Cultureel Planbureau 2000), in many cases the brands of public bureaucracies evoke feelings of powerlessness and neglect. Brands generate associations that facilitate particular socially and psychologically embedded experiences. Another example is the association of change that Barack Obama used in his campaign for the US presidential elections in 2008.

Brands also help to differentiate products from their competitors by coupling specific symbolic or experiential features to a product. In the BMW example, a BMW is not just a car; it is a car for successful people. This allows the company to sell the car for a premium price (De Chernatony and Dall'Olmo Riley 1998). Actually, this can also be seen clearly with city branding, which is applied to distinguish one city from another by giving it an image and "feel" of its own.

1.3 GOVERNANCE IN NETWORKS

Governance is a central concept in this book, but its meaning is not always clear because unfortunately governance is given many different meanings in the literature. It is important to establish how the term governance and the related term governance networks are used in this book.

What Is Governance?

In his widely cited article, Rhodes (1996) provides six different interpretations of the word governance. His overview of governance covers corporate governance, new public management, good governance as a socio-cybernetic system, governance as a self-organizing network, and other aspects. Others have built on Rhodes' definitions, adding meanings such as multi-level governance and market governance (see Frederickson 2005; Bekkers et al. 2007). Looking more closely at all the interpretations, we see four major definitions that dominate the literature (Kooiman 1993; Rhodes 1996; Pierre and Peters 2000; Frederickson 2005; Osborne 2006; Sørensen and Torfing 2007):

1. Governance as *good governance* or *corporate governance*. In this view, governance refers to the principles of a properly functioning public administration. Such an administration is characterized by the fair treatment of citizens and an unambiguous organization that adheres to the basic principles of the rule of law. The emphasis here is on the operation of government, rather than the manner in which it is organized.

2. Governance as *new public management* or *market governance* (Osborne and Gaebler 1992; Kettl 2000; Fenger and Bekkers 2007). Central to this approach is improving government performance and accountability. Under this definition, the role of government should be to steer rather than to row (Osborne and Gaebler 1992). The focus of government should be to set goals, and not on the implementation process. Policy implementation is best left to other organizations or separate public agencies that can be held accountable through the use of clear performance indicators and other market mechanisms. This definition of governance is similar to that of new public management, which stresses that governments should guide at a distance, using performance indicators and market mechanisms to arrange services and secure policy outputs.

3. Governance as *multi-level governance* or *inter-governmental relations*. In some studies, governance is described as multi-layer government or inter-governmental governance. The common theme in this diverse body of literature is the difficulty of achieving results in a multi-actor setting. This literature stresses that co-production among public actors is needed to address all aspects of societal problems because these problems tend to cross the boundaries of public organizations and their hierarchical levels (for example environmental and pollution issues that cross administrative borders and have economic and political consequences) (Bache and Flinders 2004; Agranoff and McGuire 2003; Hooghe and Marks 2002).

4. Governance as *network governance* (self-steering or non-self-steering). In some parts of the governance literature, governance and the network concept are strongly related (Kooiman 1993; Rhodes 1996; Kickert et al. 1997; Sørenson and Torfing 2007). Governance takes place within networks of public and non-public actors, and the interaction between these groups makes processes complex and difficult to manage. Consequently, different steering and management strategies are required compared to more classical approaches. The focus here

is on the complex interaction process and negotiation in a network of governmental organizations and other organizations, both private and not-for-profit.

Although these are very different conceptions of governance, they share some common elements on which we base the approach to governance that we take in this book. All perspectives on governance strongly emphasize the process of governing rather than the structure of government, and emphasize the limits of governmental power. This supports the notion of a shift in government—from organizational and uni-centric power to multi-centered processes of interaction between actors through which outcomes are achieved. As Pierre and Peters (2000, 194) state, "The strength of the state has become contextual and entrepreneurial rather than, as was previously the case, something derived from the constitutional and legal strength of the state institutions." Governance involves a shift from uni-centric steering by government to governing in pluriform coalitions between public and private parties, as well as citizens (Kooiman 2003; Stoker 1998). This does not mean that governmental actors do not seek to impose control, but their wish for authoritative action is constrained because of their dependence on others (Stoker 1998).

Governance is thus the process that takes place in governance networks of interdependent actors. We then use the term governance network to describe public policymaking and implementation through a web of relationships between government, business, and civil society actors. We consider phenomena like public–private partnerships or interactive policymaking as specific forms of governance networks. Governance networks are based on interdependencies, which are not necessarily equitable, between public, private, and civil society actors.

By stressing the aspect of interaction between multiple actors, we wish to steer away from the danger of seeing everything as governance. In our approach, good governance and corporate governance are about management in a bureaucratic setting, often in a fairly hierarchical way. Public services such as tax collection or social military service are often organized in classical bureaucracies. These are driven by classical principles of good public organization and bureaucracy. We see this as part of the classical government perspective rather than a governance perspective. New Public Management is also mainly about improving the existing bureaucracy of public organizations. Steering at a distance, using performance indicators and market mechanisms, and separating policy and implementation are all practices implemented to improve a bureaucracy's functioning by reducing it and/or binding its functioning to clear market incentives. New Public Management also emphasizes central steering; central government should set clear goals, steer with cleverly designed incentives, and then leave implementation to other organizations (Osborne and Gaebler 1992; Hood 1991). Governance, in contrast, tends to emphasize the horizontal relationships between governmental organizations and other organizations. In our view, governance is not a-political or technocratic, but inherently political. Governance processes are about reconciling different values as well as the different actors representing those values. Governance processes also involve struggles about the values represented in decision making and policy outcomes. This is precisely what makes them so complex and difficult to resolve with our classical managerial instruments and skills. One could even say that, in governance processes, politics is dissolved or displaced from the classical political institutions in a network of actors (Koppenjan and Klijn 2004; Klijn and Skelcher 2007).[2] Also, we wish to stress that, although governance implies that governmental actors are unable to force solutions on other actors, it does not mean that all actors are equal or that there are no power differences. Power differences are connected to the resources held by actors and the dependency relation between them. The dependencies in governance processes are often a-symmetrical: actor A depends more on actor B than the other way around (Kickert et al. 1997). As we will see in the next section, the existence of interdependencies means that public parties need to involve other parties in governance networks. They use brands in order to communicate and provide attractive images to appeal to other parties.

1.4 WHY ACTORS USE BRANDING IN CONTEMPORARY GOVERNANCE PROCESSES

We have described the upsurge of branding, especially in political branding and city branding, but so far we have not explored why branding is increasingly being applied in governance processes. So why do we see growing attention being paid to branding in governance processes? Why is branding applied by politicians and public managers? Explanations can be sought in: (1) the nature of current governance processes and (2) wider societal changes such as mediatization and information overload.

Changing Characteristics of Governance Processes

The character of modern governance processes itself makes branding an attractive strategy in governance. Modern governance processes show some significant changes in the way governments operate and their dependency on a large number of societal actors.

1. *Dependency and attracting stakeholders to governance processes*: Governments have to charm and appeal to other actors because governance processes can no longer be managed by governmental actors only. In urban governance for example, private investors and developers play a crucial role by providing necessary financial resources and knowledge. Citizens are also important, because they can block plans or provide local knowledge. Governments depend more and more on other actors in forming and realizing public policy (Scharpf 1978;

Rhodes 1997; Agranoff and McGuire 2001). None of the actors has sufficient resources and power to implement policies on its own. Not even the government can implement its policies top down without support from the others. To realize their goals, governmental organizations, but also the other stakeholders, need to motivate other parties to participate and invest in governance processes. Brands and branding can contribute to motivating actors to participate and bind them, as we argue in Chapter 4.

2. *Decreasing loyalty among stakeholders and voters*: The dependency on other stakeholders is enhanced by another development, and that is that governance processes are no longer characterized by the solid and permanent coalitions that could be found in, for example, "iron triangles" or "policy communities" (Jordan 1990; Rhodes 1997). Policymaking takes place in ad hoc coalitions that are formed flexibly and pragmatically, depending on the specific issue, specific preferences, and availability and resources of parties (Van Tatenhove et al. 2000). Loyalty to fixed coalitions of stakeholders has been replaced by more fluid alliances. In the political domain, a decreasing loyalty to political parties and political leaders has been witnessed. Governance processes take place in an individualized world where behavioral patterns of citizens have become less connected to traditional institutions such as political parties, labor unions, or churches. Citizens have become less loyal to such institutions, and they choose flexibly which politicians or policy initiatives they support (Sociaal Cultureel Planbureau 2000, 2009). There is a diminishing membership of political parties in Western Europe, and declining party identification (see Sociaal Cultureel Planbureau 2000; Bennett 2009; Lees-Marshment 2009). These developments mean that public managers and politicians need other ways to bind stakeholders and voters. Branding provides them with such a new instrument. Brands are used to appeal to stakeholders and enroll and bind them in governance processes. Political parties have built brands so as to enhance brand loyalty (Needham 2006) and construct an identity with which voters can identify.

3. *Governance involves a wide variety of perceptions*: Governance often involves many actors who have different perceptions of the problem and the desirable solution. This has increased with growing individualization, and the resultant variety of values makes it more difficult to achieve agreement in governance processes. These processes are therefore complex; given their dependency on stakeholders, public managers in governance processes need to pay careful attention to creating convergence in perceptions. Symbols that can bridge different opinions and facilitate joint meaning-making play an important role in this context.

4. *Governance and the penetration of popular culture into political culture*: Governance takes place in the context of a political culture that

has become penetrated by popular culture and vice versa (Richards 2009). It has become common for political executives and politicians to participate in popular television programs to win support for their policies, or just to be remembered by the electorate. Politicians are being followed by journalists from newspapers and glamour magazines in the very same way as celebrities from the world of sports or pop music. More often than not, citizens approach the political in the same way as they approach the popular; politicians and political events are assessed and evaluated in terms similar to those used to assess and evaluate popular culture. Style and emotions—important yardsticks in popular culture—have become crucial aspects in citizens' evaluation of politicians and political events also (Ewen 1988; Corner and Pels 2003). Branding can provide actors with a strategy for managing image and communicating style and emotion to the outside world.

But changes in governance processes are not the only explanation for the upsurge of branding. Branding strategies in governance processes can also be linked to three major and interrelated developments in our modern society: the growing importance of media in everyday life, the development of a visual culture, and the phenomenon of information overload.

Towards a Media Society?

Many authors have described how we are moving towards a visual culture (see e.g. Rose 2001; Sturken and Cartwright 2001). Visual media such as television, movies, and the Internet now reach masses of people. Public opinion is formed not so much by policy documents or official press releases as by images that find their way to the public in diverse media. This is strengthened by the fact that a growing number of citizens no longer obtain information from newspapers or written documents, but from TV or the Internet (Bennett 2009).

Images play a crucial role in communication about policy problems. The solid, rational argumentation of policy documents and the discursive eloquence of public speeches are often pushed aside by visual symbols and image events (Delicath and Deluca 2003). Mirzoeff (1998) argues that public administration has undergone the following changes under the influence of visual culture: (1) visual images are becoming more common in the public sphere; (2) knowledge and understanding of the administrative and political system are developing more through visual aids; (3) interaction between the public and administration and politics is becoming more constructed via visual experiences (media events on television, pictures of disasters, bloopers of politicians on the Internet, and so on). As we elaborate in Chapter 2 and Chapter 5, brands can form symbols and images in people's minds. Summarizing, brands are information carriers that thrive in the context of a visual culture in which media attention plays an important role.

A related feature of the wide availability of mass media and the Internet is the phenomenon of information overload (Klapp 1986; Wurman 1989). Information overload refers to the idea that people face more information than they can process and understand. The problem is no longer a lack of information, but an excess of information. New information is being produced rapidly and massively in knowledge societies, and it is also widely available due to mass media and the Internet. Also, information is coming in via more and more new channels such as email and RSS feeds. Information overload makes it difficult to take decisions and may even impoverish the quality of decisions. In dealing with information overload, people need to selectively attend to information. There is an abundance of information and a limited capacity to focus on multiple sources of information. It has become important to allocate attention, which is scarce, efficiently.

Thus information overload gives rise to an economy of attention. Information overload is found widely in the public sector. However, it is not only public managers and politicians that face this overload of information coming from a multitude of mass media and other sources; the general public face it also. Important questions that then arise include how to process the incoming information and how to reach, for example, the general public or fellow public managers. In this context, many public managers search for easily processed images that catch public attention. Brands are images that can function as heuristic tools through which public managers and citizens can process, for example, complex place identities, or policies.

Conclusion: Branding to Influence Perceptions, Bind Stakeholders, and Address Media

If we look at the explanations as to why branding is used in governance processes, we see that branding is strongly connected to three important aspects of governance:

1. the framing and managing of policy problems and policy solutions,
2. the activation and binding of actors to the governance process, and
3. communication to the wider environment via the media.

It is widely acknowledged that actors in governance processes have different perceptions, and that it is essential to bring together these different perceptions and find solutions that accommodate different values. But governance processes are also about mobilizing stakeholders with resources that are crucial to the process. Thus governance involves activating actors, but also connecting them to each other, and binding them to the governance process (Scharpf 1978; Koppenjan and Klijn 2004).

The existing literature on public administration and public management, however, has not paid that much attention to the relation of governance processes with the outside world, especially not when it comes to the influence of the media. This contrasts with the more classical political science research on agenda setting that extensively discussed how policy problems entered the political agenda, and how mobilizing the broader public and media influenced that (see Cobb and Elder 1983; Kingdon 1984). The media have become prominent, and actually one of the main factors by which external attention and pressure penetrates into governance networks. This book certainly has to deal with the media aspects of branding.

1.5   THE STRUCTURE OF THIS BOOK

This book elaborates the use of brands and branding in governance processes. To start with, in Chapter 2 we explore what brands and branding really mean and what makes them suitable for using in governance processes. We dig into the meaning of brands, we explain the difference between branding and framing—a well-known phenomenon in governance processes—and we explain that branding can be seen as a strategy for managing perceptions. We also elaborate on various forms of branding.

After this, we explore the importance of branding in governance processes. We do this by connecting branding to the three main dimensions of governance formulated in the previous section: framing and influencing perceptions (Chapter 3), connecting and binding stakeholders (Chapter 4), and dealing with the outside world, especially the media (Chapter 5). In Chapter 3, we explore why branding is an interesting phenomenon in the light of framing policy problems and solutions. Chapter 4 explains why branding is relevant for activating and binding actors to governance processes. Chapter 5 deals with external pressure and the media influence on governance processes. It explains the value of brands and branding to cope with this.

In Chapter 6 we look at branding as a management strategy. How does it distinguish itself from other governance management strategies? For that, we explore the literature about management in governance processes and explain what branding strategies add to this. Chapter 7 deals with the risks and limitation of branding in governance processes. We end with conclusions and reflections in Chapter 8.

2   The Many Faces of Branding
Definitions, Functions, and Forms

2.1   WHAT IS A BRAND, AND WHAT IS BRANDING?

We have seen in the previous chapter that brands are being used more and more in governance processes, but it is not always clear whether we are dealing with a clear example of branding. Is it branding when a municipality creates a new website for their new project in the inner city where they are reconstructing the central district area? Is it branding when they construct logos and advertise the project by telling the citizens what this project will deliver to the city? And is it branding when the municipality together with various stakeholders construct a specific image of the project? And in what way does a brand really differ from the classical policy document in which governmental actors used to communicate their plans? To understand brands and branding we must first sort out what they really are and how they differ from more classical ways of managing perceptions in governance processes.

What Is a Brand?

A first step in defining brands is to clarify that, as has become clear in the first chapter, we approach brands as symbols (see also Arvidsson 2006; Danesi 2006). As Danesi (2006) argues, a brand is a sign with a denotative function that identifies an object, and a connotative function that evokes associations through which an object is imbued with meaning. Thus, on the one hand brands refer to something tangible like a commercial product (beer, perfume), a place (Amsterdam, New York), or a person (a rock star, a politician). As we show in this book, it is also possible to brand policies (for example as innovative or green) or governance processes (for instance as joined-up governance). On the other hand, however, brands are more than something tangible, because they stimulate associations that enrich the product. In the case of a perfume, the brand enriches the perfume for example with notions of attractiveness and sex appeal. In the case of a politician, the brand may add notions of hope and change.

It must be stressed, however, that there is a difference between brands and products. Brands are symbols, which is not the same thing as the branded object or product. Thus, a brand may influence the meaning that people give to a product, and a product may influence how people perceive a brand, but they are clearly different things.[1]

Defining a brand as a sign or symbol is a first step towards delineating what a brand is, but it is insufficient. There are many symbols that are not brands, for example pictorials on traffic signs and keyboards, or coats of arms on flags. Therefore it is important to be more precise about what brands are. We argue that brands are a specific kind of symbol with four particular characteristics (see e.g. Arvidsson 2006; Batey 2008; Blichfeldt 2005; Kotler et al. 1999). Brands:

- give meaning to something; that is, they construct a web of associations that create meaning with consumers, voters, tourists, or other groups of audiences reached by the brand;
- add value to the branded product or object. Brands enhance the value of the product or the tangible asset in general. A Gucci bag is not especially valuable as a functional bag. What makes it worth the price, at least in the eyes of many consumers, is the added value of the Gucci brand;
- distinguish the branded object or product from similar things especially from "competitors," which can for example be similar products (other perfumes), other persons (other politicians), or similar places (other attractive cities);
- have a concrete, visible manifestation in the form of a sign, a design, or a name. The visible manifestation is essential to gain attention. It is also important for distinguishing the branded product. To give an example, the particular design of Citroën cars and the logo on the car make the brand visible and distinguish Citroën cars from other cars. However, visual manifestations of brands appear to be less dominant in governance than in the private sphere. Part of the reason for this is that it is not always easy to come up with clear logos or visuals of policy content. At the same time, policy content can be branded with the aid of visual manifestations, as the examples of Tony Blair's "New Labour" and other logos of British political parties prove (see Figure 2.1). The New Labour brand illustrates how brands help to differentiate a policy or policy ideas from other ideas. The New Labour brand differentiated the party from Labour as it had been for years, and also from the Conservative Party. New Labour was different from "old Labour"; the latter was closely linked to the unions and put a strong emphasis on fighting social inequalities. New Labour was also positioned as different from the Conservatives in that it did not concentrate as heavily on privatization, lower taxes, and labor flexibility as the Conservatives did. The name New Labour illustrates the

discursive manifestation of a brand, and how important this is to distinguish the brand (from Labour in this case) (see Figure 2.1).

Brands help to differentiate products from their competitors by coupling specific symbolic or experiential features to a product. This can be seen in one of the forms of branding that is often applied in the public sector: city branding. City brands aim to distinguish one city from another by giving it an image and "feel" of its own. Paris is not just a city; it is a city of romance. New York is not just another big city; it is a main financial center in the world. Branding the city in this way adds value; in the New York example, it allows owners of real estate, especially in the financial heart of the city, to ask a premium price for their buildings and apartments. It also attracts functions that fit into the brand and thus generates a kind of clustering where firms can profit from the fact that other firms are present.

The relevance of visible elements of brands and differentiating products from others has been acknowledged in the literature. In their standard text, Kotler et al. (1999, 571) describe a brand as "a name, term, sign, symbol

Figure 2.1   Visible manifestations of brands of British political parties (Labour, Liberal Democrats, and Conservatives).

or design, or a combination of these, intended to identify the goods or services of one seller or group of sellers and to differentiate them from those of competitors."[2] With Kotler and colleagues, we acknowledge the importance of a name, term, or sign that identifies the product. However, brands as symbols should not be reduced to visual or material manifestations of the brand such as names and signs. We follow Kapferer (1992) who argues that the crucial element of a brand is that it gives meaning to the product and defines its identity. He remarks that a brand is more than its component parts, such as the brand name, the logo, or design, although these are of course part of the brand (see also Danesi 2006). With Kapferer, we want to go beyond the material and visible manifestations of a brand and also include more immanent aspects such as the identity and meaning of brands. We therefore approach a brand not simply as a slogan or a logo, but as a symbolic construct that identifies something and gives meaning to it (in order to add value and differentiate it). The logo is a material or visual manifestation of the brand in the form of a pictorial; a slogan is a discursive manifestation of the brand. As explained more elaborately in section 2.3 on meaning-making, all material, visual, and discursive manifestations of the brand, as well as the product that is being branded, influence the meaning of the brand. Brands imbue products with meaning, but products also influence the meaning that people give to the brand. For example, if a certain company keeps producing low-quality products, the brand will come to be seen as a low-quality brand.

We can conclude that a brand needs material, visual, or discursive manifestations in order to gain attention and distinguish products, but it also has aspects such as an identity that go beyond directly visible manifestations. This element also needs to be included in our definition of brands. But before arriving at our definition of branding, there is one more issue we want to discuss, and that is that branding is a deliberately organized process.

The Deliberate Character of Branding

Kavaratzis (2008, 53), in a discussion on city branding, explains that branding involves selecting and associating attributes to add value to the basic product or service; it involves deliberate attempts to influence how citizens interpret a brand and evaluate a branded product. Note that the goal of branding may be to give meaning to a product, but also to give meaning to the brand itself. Since brands have themselves become valuable assets (see Kotler et al. 1999; Kapferer 1992), it has become more important to influence perceptions of these brands deliberately.

Conceptualizing branding as a *deliberate process* implies that branding should be distinguished from unconscious processes of meaning-making. By reserving the term branding for consciously undertaken activities, we wish to separate branding from processes of identity formation and unconscious forms of invocation of meaning. This is not to say that these processes cannot influence brands and branding processes in some ways, but they are not in themselves branding. In this way, we aim to prevent the term branding from acquiring a very wide meaning, overlapping with other terms, and losing its specific meaning. Reserving the term branding for conscious forms of positioning an object or subject implies, for example, that we do not consider criminal behavior in neighborhoods that influences the brand of that neighborhood as part of the branding process. We consider such behavior as a factor that influences branding.[3]

A Definition of Brands in Governance

Thus, for a good definition of a brand, we have to acknowledge brands as symbols that are created deliberately and take into account the four characteristics that help to differentiate brands from other symbols. Kotler et al.'s (1999) frequently used definition cited above may serve as a base because it points out a number of important characteristics of brands. However, we need to adapt the definition to make it fit for governance processes. Therefore, our definition is not restricted to products (goods and services) as some of the definitions in the marketing literature are. In governance processes, the branded object can also be a policy process, a project, or a coalition of parties. Our definition may also differ from definitions that stress competitiveness to the extent that some of the generally used definitions in the marketing literature do (e.g. Kotler et al. 1999).

Taking into account important characteristics of governance processes and brands, we arrive at the following definition of brands used in governance processes.

A brand is a symbolic construct that consists of a name, term, sign, symbol, or design, or a combination of these, created deliberately to identify a phenomenon and differentiate it from similar phenomena by adding particular meaning to it.

2.2 FORMS OF BRANDING

Now that we have defined brands, we can look at the objects and subjects to which branding can apply. This clarifies the reach that brands can have and also what branding in governance processes can imply.

In the private sector, branding is mostly about branding tangible goods or products, but also services or service processes. In addition, a wide range of objects and subjects are branded; for example holiday destinations, sportsmen, pop stars, certified processes, and corporate organizations (Grainge 2008; Kotler et al. 1999; Schultz et al. 2000; Smart 2005). Drawing on marketing literature (Balmer 2006; Kotler et al. 1999), we

Table 2.1   Five Forms of Branding

Form of Branding	Goods Branding	Process Branding	Person Branding	Organizational Branding	Place Branding
Object of branding	tangible goods or products	interactive policy making, participatory projects, integrated environmental assessments	person	(corporate) organization	geographical place
Example in the private sector	cars, jeans	ISO 9000, certified quality management systems	David Beckham	Google, Nike, Tata	Bahamas
Example in public governance processess	infrastructural works, e.g. the Øresund Bridge connecting Denmark and Sweden	joined-up governance	Silvio Berlusconi, Barack Obama	Dutch Tax Organization	New York (I love New York campaign)

analytically distinguish five major categories of branded objects that can also be found in governance processes: tangible goods, processes, persons, organizations, and places (see Table 2.1).

The table presents examples of each type of branding in the private and the public sphere. We briefly discuss each form of branding as it appears in the public sector and provide short vignettes of the most important ones.

1. *Branding tangible goods* is less common in public governance processes than in the private sector, where it is the most important form of branding. The production of tangible goods is less central in the public sector than it is in the private sector, although the public sector does produce tangible goods such as passports, (subsidized) artworks, and infrastructural goods such as roads, railroads, bridges, and tunnels. In most cases, it is not deemed necessary to brand public sector goods because of the absence of market competition. However, in several cases, infrastructure goods are branded as icons of cities, like the Øresund Bridge in Copenhagen–Malmö (see vignette) or the Brooklyn Bridge in New York.

Vignette: Øresund Bridge

The Øresund Bridge lies between Denmark and Sweden. To be more specific, it forms a connection between Copenhagen and Malmö. The bridge combines a railroad and a four-lane road. During the planning of the bridge in the 1990s, its supporters argued that the bridge would be important to increase commercial exchange and economic growth in the region, but for a long time a majority of the public were opposed to it. From then on, the bridge was actively branded as being more than a simple bridge. It is now branded as connecting two countries and, more than that, connecting the people from the two countries. The branding builds on the idea of unity among Nordic countries, and the design of the bridge is presented as rooted in Nordic building traditions. The bridge is presented as more than a designed structure of concrete and steel; it is presented as an experience: "The experience of crossing the Øresund Bridge is thus enhanced by the architectural impression of cohesion and simplicity with the high bridge as the towering symbol of the entire link" (http://uk.Øresund sbron.com/page/367). The positioning of the bridge has been achieved by connecting the design of the bridge with socio-political goals, namely, the linking of two countries and enhancing cohesion among Nordic countries (see e.g. Hospers 2006; Pedersen 2004).

2. *Branding processes* in the public sector can refer to various aspects. In the first place, they may pertain to the branding of services that are provided by governments. Services like education, social security, health services, elderly care, or tax collection (although that may not be a service that citizens particularly like) are an important part of what governments offer to citizens by means of the public sector. A wide range of public services can be and are branded, such as educational services or public safety. Besides services, it is also possible to brand policies or even decision-making processes themselves. In the latter case, it is mainly the style of decision making or policymaking that is branded. For instance, decision-making processes may be branded as "innovative," "joined-up," or "interactive with citizens"; but the content of policies can also be branded as the example of the Third Way shows. The next vignette shows how the city of Rotterdam branded its policies for dealing with urban problems as a particularly innovative and daring approach. The focus of the brand was on policy style.

Vignette: The Rotterdam Approach

In 2002, the Dutch city of Rotterdam experienced a major political change when a new populist party, called Livable Rotterdam, became the biggest political party in the city. This meant a major change in the city where Labor had been the largest political party since 1945 (see also Noordergraaf and Vermeulen 2010; Uitermark and Duyvendak 2008). When Livable Rotterdam came to power, they changed the policy approach of the municipality quite radically. They put a strong focus on implementation and accountability. They formulated targets and developed elaborate monitoring systems (for example the Safety Index), which they used to explicate what had been accomplished (see also Noordergraaf and Vermeulen 2010). The approach was branded as the "Rotterdam Approach," meaning a daring and vigorous approach in which no instrument is left unused for solving persistent problems. If measures that can help to solve persistent problems are forbidden, then the law should be changed! The Rotterdam Approach also means an anti-bureaucracy attitude, no-nonsense, and straightforwardness combined with an aversion to intellectual discussions. The slogan that is often associated with the Rotterdam Approach is "No words but deeds."[4] As we further explain in Chapter 3, the Rotterdam Approach brand was also used to present and brand particular measures taken by the municipality as daring (instead of for example harsh and illegal).

3. *Branding organizations* takes the organization as a whole as an important platform for identity formation and differentiation, in addition to the services or policies it develops (cf. e.g. Balmer 2006; Schultz et al. 2000). Branding of public organizations can refer to the branding of ministries, municipal organizations, agencies, or political parties.

Vignette: Dutch Tax Organization

The Dutch Tax Organization has tried to rebrand itself to overcome its negative image as a bureaucratic organization. Aware that tax organizations are widely disliked because they collect money from individuals and organizations, the Dutch Tax Organization chose a slogan that acknowledges this: "We can't make it more fun, but we can make it easier." It indicates that, although the tax organization requires its customers to engage in work that will never be fun (filling out forms so that one has to pay the government), it tries to make that work as easy as possible. The slogan, intensively communicated by a massive advertising campaign, implicitly communicates three core values—helpfulness, empathy, and service orientation—thus helping to create a new web of associations around the tax organization. The branding was supported by a switch by the tax organization to electronic forms that could be downloaded from the Internet to make the process of filling in the form much easier.

4. *Branding people* in the public sector generally refers to political lead-ers, for example Tony Blair or George W. Bush. In contrast to the pri-vate sector, public managers normally stay out of the glare of publicity since they "serve" the political leaders. However, branding is increas-ingly being used by a wider range of professionals to market them-selves (Lair et al. 2005). Public managers and professionals in general brand themselves to communicate their strengths, position themselves within their organization, and enhance their career. Finally, branding can also be relied upon by other public figures, such as the late Prin-cess Diana.

Vignette: Silvio Berlusconi, prime minister of Italy

Mr. Berlusconi exemplifies a leader who is able to deliver an emo-tion that people can identify with. Even though it is very difficult for Berlusconi, as it is for many politicians who deal with numerous contradictory demands, to communicate a coherent message, he has created a coherent brand. What Berlusconi has understood well is the importance of the aspirational and the evocation of images of the good life.[5] Central to the Berlusconi brand is "sweetening." Ber-lusconi is able to "present the world as a better, happier and sweeter place. Like McDonald's or Disney, he offers this as a possible experi-ence. As in the case of brand management, it is the emotional level that counts, the ability to appropriate affect" (Arvidsson 2006, 92). Other important elements of his brand are continuity and reliabil-ity, in the sense that Berlusconi wants to assure voters that he will always be the same and that he will provide continuity for Italy. This strategy has been especially successful in the Italian context where since the Second World War governments have served less than one year on average. In order to build and maintain his brand of conti-nuity and the world as a sweet place, Berlusconi carefully manages his (physical) appearance. He underwent plastic surgery in order to look young and the same forever, and avoid associations with decay. Another element of Berlusconi's brand management is his intensive reliance on and use of the media, especially through the television channels that he owns. Berlusconi has used his newspapers and tele-vision stations to widely advertise his leadership and his political party, Forza Italia. Critics argue that Berlusconi finds it more impor-tant to communicate his policies in (his own) television studios than in parliament. They argue that Berlusconi's media-centered way of policymaking has a negative impact on processes of democratic control, especially in combination with the high degree of control that Berlusconi wields over the media (see e.g. Ginsborg 2005; Stille 2006). The Berlusconi example highlights the importance of the media in branding. It also draws attention to risks and drawbacks of branding. We deal further with branding and the media in Chapter 5, and we elaborate on (democratic) risks of branding in Chapter 7.

5. *Branding places* focuses on geographical locations, such as nations, cities, regions, and communities. It is variously referred to as place branding (e.g. Kavaratzis and Ashworth 2005; Gould and Skinner 2007), city branding, or location branding (e.g. Hankinson 2001). This type of branding is usually aimed at enhancing the attractiveness of places to stimulate corporate investors, firms, or individuals to settle in the place or to come to the place and spend money (tourists). It is also aimed at creating a special image of the place that distinguishes it from other places. Place branding normally involves public and private actors. For example, when a city is branded to attract tourists or investors, the tourist board, hotels, museums, and the municipality are usually involved in the branding process.

Vignette: New York

Since the 1970s, New York has launched several branding campaigns to change the image of the city in the minds of potential visitors, investors, and other business people. Probably the most famous one has been the "I ♥ NY" campaign (*I love New York*). This campaign was launched in 1977 to counter the negative image that New York had developed as an asphalt jungle and ungovernable city (Greenberg 2008). It was felt that the negative image had a large negative impact on New York's status as a global financial center and that it hampered efforts to improve the position of the city. The campaign aimed to attract financial corporations to the city and spur economic growth again. City branding as applied in New York is a strategy of both positioning the city in a positive way through communication and adapting the governance of the city to make the brand come true. Through television and the print media, the city was positioned as a rich cultural place and global financial center. According to critics, the branding of New York has been a very selective presentation of the city: "The representation of the city in the I love NY campaign was limited to the skyline and landmarks of Manhattan, the lights of Broadway, and glamorous dining and shopping" (Greenberg 2008, 234). Greenberg stresses how the city started to ignore poor and working-class people, and aimed at attracting more affluent people and large corporations. Or as she remarks: "[T]hrough a combination of marketing and pro-business restructuring, this model has been successfully branded, forever changing the image and material reality of NY City, and providing a powerful base from which the neoliberal ideology could spread its wings and rise nationally and internationally . . . " (Greenberg 2008, 232).

So we can conclude that branding can be applied to many objects and processes; and the five forms of branding can be applied in both the public sector and the private sector. Despite the similarities when it comes to the kind of objects, there are differences between branding in the private and public sector. The context, in particular, is different in the two sectors. In the public sphere, branding not only refers to selling products and images that endow these products with additional qualities, but is also about choosing appropriate problem definitions and selecting different solutions; this, of course, has political implications. For example, the branding of the Third Way was not a neutral activity. Rather, it emphasized particular values, problem definitions, and solutions. Public policymaking involves value struggles among many different actors, and these may result in a process where the brand is contested.

2.3   HOW BRANDS CREATE MEANING BY TRIGGERING ASSOCIATIONS

Having defined what a brand is and having looked at various forms of branding, we now turn to what in our opinion is a crucial issue in branding; that is, that branding is a process in which a phenomenon is distinguished and increased in value by giving the phenomenon symbolic meaning that is valuable in the psychological and social life of actors (cf. Arvidsson 2006; Danesi 2006). But how does this process of giving symbolic meaning actually work? This question is addressed in this section.

Creating Meaning as a Neurological and Psychological Process

At a fundamental level, branding involves the evocation of positive associations with a particular phenomenon. Branding is about connecting a particular phenomenon, for example a policy or a coalition, with particular ideas by stimulating or facilitating particular associations over others. To clarify this, we must turn to the genesis of associations in the brain. Every encounter with a brand or a product produces particular associations. Over time, during multiple encounters, a web of associations develops in the brain. This involves the reinforcement of particular connections between neurons. Neurons that store particular sounds, visual impressions, or words become more strongly connected to the brand. In a neuropsychological sense a brand is a "totality of stored synaptic connections" (Batey 2008, 5).

So branding is about consciously connecting a phenomenon with particular words, images, emotions, ideas, in order to facilitate the development of particular webs of associations in the brain. To that end, logos, wordmarks, slogans, and visual images, but also music, can be used. Branding a political party, for example, may involve showing the party leader accompanied by and listening to the general public, thus forging associations with the populace and caring about them. An example of the use of music to create associations was the former US president Bill Clinton who used the Fleetwood Mac song "Don't Stop Thinking about Tomorrow" in his presidential campaign of 1992. It created various strong associations, like youthfulness (associated with pop music), it appealed to a generation who recognized the song and had positive memories of the period when the song was a hit in the 1970s (1977), and last but not least it set Clinton apart as someone from a new generation of leaders who had grown up after the Second World War. Although several advisors told Clinton not to use the tune, it was a huge success and was used on several occasions later on when Clinton made important public appearances, like his presentation at the 2008 Democratic convention when Obama was elected as presidential candidate (see the various films on YouTube).

Box 2.1   Brands as Persuasive Communication: How the Message of Brands Is Processed

Branding can be seen as a form of persuasive communication in the sense that it aims to change perceptions about some object or subject. Branding therefore relies heavily on quick processing of messages, rather than elaborate and systematic processing of messages. This can be explained further through the so-called dual process models that have been developed in social psychology: the elaboration likelihood model developed by Petty and Cacioppo, and the heuristic value model developed by Chaiken and colleagues (Nienhuis 1998). Dual process models argue that there are two routes to persuasion, namely, one route via systematic and elaborate processing of messages, and another route via heuristic and quick processing of the messages. If actors are interested in a subject, they will be motivated to attend to messages on the subject and follow the central route of systematic processing of the message content. This means that they will carefully go through the message, analyze its arguments, and consider the arguments in the light of arguments already known. They will weigh the quality of the arguments. The processing of the arguments may bring new thoughts and perceptions.

   In the other case, when actors are not interested in a subject or occupied with many subjects that demand attention at the same time, they will rather follow the peripheral route. This route implies a quick scan of the message by assessing things such as the number of arguments, feelings of affect, or the attractiveness and expertise of the source. The actor uses heuristics such as "consensus about a message implies that the message is correct," or "the more arguments the stronger the message." Notably, the content of the message is less important in the peripheral route than it is in the central route. Other things such as characteristics of the sender also play a role in influencing perceptions through the

continued

peripheral route. Both the central and the peripheral routes can have an effect on perceptions. However, experiments have shown that a change in perceptions resulting from the systematic processing of information in the central route is (a) relatively durable, (b) predictive of behavior, and (c) resistant to contra-arguments (Nienhuis 1998).

It must be noted that the central and peripheral routes should be seen as ends on a continuum, on which the degree of processing arguments differs from strong to weak and the influence of peripheral elements varies from weak to strong. The two routes are not mutually exclusive; and actors process messages through a combination of systematic processing and quickly assessing peripheral cues (Nienhuis 1998; Van Meegeren 1997). Some researchers have argued that pure systematic processing of arguments never takes place in practice; actors are always influenced by affective reactions that they develop even before they can start weighing arguments (see e.g. Zajonc 1980).

The next question that we want to answer is how these associations can be facilitated. We argue that emotive stimuli and visual stimuli are crucial in stimulating associations in branding processes. It is then repetition of the message that ensures that associations are remembered and filed away in the memory. Consequently, it is the repeated communication of brand elements such as slogans and the underlying brand values that is very important.

Branding is about connecting a product with psychologically and socially meaningful ideas to make the product psychologically and socially more relevant to people and increase its value. The example of the branding of AXE deodorant may clarify this. In its advertisements, AXE hardly mentions the nice odor of the deodorant or other characteristics of the product itself. Instead, the message is that the deodorant increases the attractiveness and sex appeal of the user. In the AXE advertisements, male AXE users become irresistibly attractive to any ladies coming near them, drawing the ladies towards them as if they were being pulled towards the men by physical force. The advertisement associates AXE with excitement and attraction. The brand makes the AXE deodorant valuable in the sense of satisfying the human psychological need to be attractive and giving a pleasurable emotional experience of excitement and liking. The case exemplifies the importance of emotive stimuli in branding, and it makes clear that the rational component of brands need not be the most important. No one really believes the claim that AXE actually attracts women, but despite that the brand still seems to work. Branding builds on the idea that emotional liking is crucial in deliberating and making choices. In that sense, ideas on branding differ from most theories about policymaking and governance, in which the rational or at least the reasonable aspect of deliberating and discussing policy content is dominant.

Brands build on the insight that, in the deliberation that forms part of planning processes, emotions "help to assign values to different options or product attributes" (O'Shaughnessy and O'Shaughnessy 2003, 28). Values or key concerns structure the relative importance of things, and emotional responses inform us about what we value (O'Shaughnessy and O'Shaughnessy 2003; Wagenaar and Cook 2003). Without emotions, it becomes very difficult to determine what is important and make up one's mind (Marcus 2000; Turner 2007). Most theories about policymaking, even those that focus on framing and discourses (see Fischer 2003; Schön and Rein 1994), tend to emphasize the fact that deliberation is about constructing logical arguments for choices and confronting these with each other (see Dryzek 2000; Hajer and Wagenaar 2003). Emotions (and power) are seen as distorting the "good process of deliberations." In a way, emotions are not "logical." Thus one can say that the role of emotions in policy processes is systematically downplayed in most public administration perspectives and governance theories. In that sense, the branding literature has something to offer for governance theories.[6] We elaborate further on this in the next section (section 2.4).

2.4   DIFFERENCES BETWEEN BRANDING, RATIONAL, AND DELIBERATIVE APPROACHES TO GOVERNANCE

Branding in governance processes is an explicit attempt to influence perceptions of involved stakeholders on crucial elements, such as the perception of the problem, solutions, the innovativeness of the policy, or the competencies of the initiator to mention a few, and this brings branding close to other well-known governance strategies like framing (Schön and Rein 1994). In this section, we deal with differences between branding and other existing strategies for managing perceptions in governance processes, in particular rational and deliberative approaches.

In traditional, rational approaches to influencing perceptions, governments use scientific research to clarify policy problems and determine possible solutions. Persuasive communication and extension are applied to disseminate research findings and policy decisions. The central aim of perception management, as understood in rational approaches, is to convince stakeholders of governmental policies using scientifically established information and planned extension (see e.g. Braybrooke and Lindblom 1963). Thus, perception management in this perspective resembles a classical form of public relations in which information is communicated only one way.

This approach to perception management has been criticized for its inability to deal with ambiguity and differing perceptions among actors in governance networks (Koppenjan and Klijn 2004). The impossibility of defining problems and solutions objectively demands approaches that help actors to reflect on their own perceptions, as well as to discuss and jointly construct new problem perceptions (Hajer and Wagenaar 2003). In this regard, the management of perceptions facilitates deliberation between actors to develop new frames and jointly accepted packages of solutions. Examples of this form of perception management include processes of reframing (Schön and Rein 1994; Lewicki et al. 2003) and integrative negotiation (Susskind and Cruikshank 1987).

Branding differs from the two forms of perception management mentioned above in several ways. First, branding emphasizes the emotional and the psychological; it is not particularly aimed at either deliberation or reason. In terms of the elaboration likelihood model developed by Petty and Cacioppo in 1986 (see Box 2.1), branding aims at the peripheral route of information processing. This route is not characterized by the systematic processing of information and rational weighing of arguments (the central route), but rather by affective and quick assessments based on heuristics.

For example, the city of Manchester was not branded primarily by providing fact sheets comparing it with other cities; the branding involved evoking an image and associating the city with such emotional, impressionistic adjectives as "exciting," "lively," and "cosmopolitan" (Bramwell and Rawding 1996; Young et al. 2006). Political leaders (e.g. the US president Barack Obama) are branded not by rationally explaining the superiority of their leadership but by associating them with broader ideals (e.g. "hope" and "change"). Thus although information and facilitating deliberation strategies can be used in branding, they are not what branding is primarily based upon. Branding is based upon creating images that evoke emotions.

Second, branding works partly through the unconscious. People are largely unaware of the associations triggered by brands, and they do not commonly deliberate about them. As sketched in section 2.2, the Italian leader Berlusconi tries to evoke images of the good life and of a better and sweeter world (Arvidsson 2006). The associations that fit his brand are triggered in both his verbal and his nonverbal communication. Again as mentioned in section 2.2, Berlusconi underwent plastic surgery in order to look young and vital, thus creating a physical appearance that is unconsciously associated with a good, vital, and healthy life.

Thus brands differ in various ways from deliberative approaches in which frames are an important concept. Box 2.2 summarizes the main differences between branding and framing.

Box 2.2   Differences between Branding and Framing

Brand or frame?

In the governance literature a frequently used concept with regard to meaning-making is the concept of "frame" (see e.g. Schön and Rein 1994; Lewicki et al. 2003). It is therefore relevant to be explicit about commonalities and differences between brands and frames. An important commonality is that both frames and brands give meaning to phenomena. When we look closer at frames and brands we see important

continued

differences however. Firstly, frames are "schemata of interpretation" (Goffman 1986) or "cognitive structures" (Dewulf et al. 2009), whereas brands are symbols that are often characterized by a visual manifestation. Frames mostly do not have a clear visual manifestation, but they do appear in verbal communication. This is related to the second difference, namely, that frames help to interpret information by fitting the information into pre-existing schemata (Dewulf et al. 2009). Framing is thus a matter of applying cognitive schemata to a situation or a phenomenon. Brands influence interpretation not by fitting information into schemata, but more by triggering webs of associations. Thirdly, differences between branding and framing can be found in their functions. Branding has the function of distinguishing a phenomenon from similar phenomena and adding value to it. The main functions of frames are in understanding and interpreting phenomena. Fourthly, brands work more through the visual and emotional, whereas framing is often more a discursive and argumentative activity. Related to this is the idea that the processing of frames in the brain relies more strongly on systematic comparison and assessing the quality of arguments in a message, whereas branding relies more on quickly and intuitively assessing how the message feels, thereby relying on peripheral cues such as the expertise of the source of the message (see also Box 2.1).

	Brand	*Frame*
Main function	Gives meaning	Gives meaning
Other function	Distinguishes and adds value	Understands and interprets
Appearance	As visual symbols	As verbal communication
Structure	Web of (cognitive) associations	(Cognitive) scheme
Processing	Peripheral route	Central route
Communication	Visual	Verbal
Logic	Emotional	Rational

To conclude this section on managing perceptions, it is the focus on the emotional and the appeal to the unconscious that distinguish branding from other approaches to governance and managing perceptions, particularly rational approaches (e.g. Braybrooke and Lindblom 1963) and most deliberative approaches that center on argumentation and conscious deliberation (e.g. Fischer 2003; Hajer and Wagenaar 2003). This also means that the branding perspective adds something to our understanding of governance. We explore that further in the next chapters by looking at what branding does to actors' perceptions (Chapter 3), by elaborating how branding contributes in activating and binding actors to governance networks (Chapter 4), and exploring how branding can facilitate communications with the outside world—especially with the media that always seem to accompany governance processes (Chapter 5).

Before proceeding to the next chapters, we deal here with one more issue that is relevant for applying the branding concept in a governance context: the issue of multiple actors giving meaning to brands. So far, we have mainly limited ourselves to the idea that brand owners and brand managers give meaning to brands, which then give meaning to branded objects; but in a governance context multiple actors may give meaning to brands.

2.6   WHO GIVES MEANING TO BRANDS: THE MULTIPLICITY OF INTERPRETATIONS IN GOVERNANCE

The facts that brands are applied to create associations, and that brands are perceptional in the sense that actors have their own perceptions of brands, also have consequences for the question of who gives meaning to brands. Especially in governance processes where many different stakeholders are involved, brands acquire their meaning in a multi-actor environment. This requires a slightly different perspective on branding than that mostly used in classical marketing approaches. Traditionally, marketing theory focused on the meaning given to a brand by marketers and brand owners (brands as communicators). Most emphasis was placed on the communicative function of brands and the value-added function. More recent marketing theory acknowledges the importance of consumers' meaning-giving processes (brands as perceptual entities).We present the two perspectives to clarify the differences (see also Hankinson 2004).

Two Perspectives on Who Gives Meaning to Brands

Brands as communicators: as communicators, brands represent a name, term, or symbol that can identify a good or service and distinguish it from other products (see also Hankinson 2004). In this perspective, the primary function of brands is to enhance the visibility and communicate the characteristics of a product, person, place, or process in a crowded and mediatized world where many things are vying for attention. This perspective is still very classical in the sense that is mainly occupied with communicating one way: from a brand to an audience. The audience is considered as more or less passive, or at least not an important element of the communication. The brand owner or brand managers develop the brand and its meaning. This meaning is communicated via advertisements and other promotional instruments.

Applying this perspective to governance processes leads to a focus on the meaning that the organizations that have developed a brand give to the brand. This perspective also emphasizes the importance of reaching the target groups and using the right communication instruments and media to do so.

Brands as perceptual entities for an audience: the second perspective is that brands appeal to the senses and perceptions of consumers, voters, residents, and all other audiences that a brand is aimed at. In this perspective, brands above all evoke sets of associations among an audience (see Batey 2008; Hankinson 2004). The perceptual function goes further than the communication function in the sense that it takes the reaction of consumers or citizens into account. Or as Hankinson (2004) argues, in this perspective the audience's perception of the brand is important, whereas in the first perspective what the brand manager wants to communicate is more important. Also, when brands are seen as perceptual entities, the communication about characteristics of branded objects such as tangible products or policies is the central function. The concept of brands as perceptual reveals how important the eye of the beholder is when it comes to the perception of products and policy content.

Within a governance context, this perspective pays attention to the stakeholders' perceptions of a branded object or subject. It allows for a multiplicity of perceptions and illuminates differences between meanings that brand managers give and meanings that others give to, for instance, branded policy processes or branded organizations.

In summary, both brand owners and other stakeholders can give meaning to brands. Stakeholders may develop relationships with brands and through this relationship they can even reconstruct the brand.

In the next section, we link the perspectives described above more closely to governance processes. The main line of our argument is that brands are usually consciously promoted by brand managers, but the fact that brands are experienced and co-produced by consumers and citizens also creates ambiguity and limits the possibilities of forming a brand in a predetermined way.

Multiple Interpretations of a Brand in Governance Processes

When actors give meaning to brands, multiple interpretations of brands develop, and perceptions of brands may become ambiguous in the sense that not every actor has the same associations and perceives the same image. In the case of brands used in governance processes, this character is even more prominent than in most commercial brands. Because there are many different types of actors present in governance networks (for example citizen groups, private actors, various public actors, various pressure groups, knowledge organizations), there is a great chance of different perceptions of the brand emerging. And the fact that public brands are often at the center of public debate contributes to the multiple meaning and multiple construction of brands in governance processes. Thus brands in governance processes are interpreted and reconstructed by multiple actors.

So brands in governance processes are directed at, and interpreted by, various actors. We explore this crucial character of brands in governance processes further in Chapter 3. This means that it not easy to consciously brand governance processes and that such brands are contested or even vulnerable to counter branding. We deal with these two topics in the next two sections.

Difficulties of Managing Brands in Governance Processes

In governance processes, authorities may try to manage the branding process and thus control who gives meaning to the brand, for example by running a branding campaign. However, apart from branding processes organized by authorities, other actors may also engage in branding activities and try to give meaning to the brand. To understand who gives meaning to brands we must therefore explore the managed attempts to include and exclude stakeholders in branding processes, and we must look at the less organized, messy processes of branding by multiple actors in the governance process.

When it comes to managing branding processes, two main approaches can be distinguished: a top-down, sales-oriented approach which we will call the instrumental approach, and a horizontal, marketing-oriented approach which we will call the interactive approach (see also Lees-Marshment 2004). We see these approaches as two ends of a continuum, with on one end the instrumental approach with relatively little stakeholder involvement, and on the other end the interactive approach with high stakeholder involvement.

The instrumental, top-down approach is primarily aimed at persuading other stakeholders and "selling" something. For example, in the case of branding a political party in a top-down way, the board of the party or a committee within the party would decide how to brand the party together with marketing experts or communication experts. Without listening to voters, they would decide what core values, symbolism, and emotional qualities to impose upon the party brand. They would then focus on communicating the quality and the (expected) performance of the party to the electorate, thereby using the party brand as a symbol and shorthand in their communications. Thus, branding is used to realize a predefined goal, in the sense of imposing particular predefined meanings and sending out preselected messages. It is an attempt at top-down meaning-making. The assumption is that voters (or other stakeholders) will select the political party (or policy plan or other branded object) with the most appealing (emotional) characteristics.

At the other end of the continuum, there is the interactive branding approach, which centers around getting to know stakeholders' needs and then creating a brand that responds to that. Branding is no longer viewed primarily as selling, but as satisfying stakeholders' needs or voters' needs (cf. Lees-Marshment 2004; Kotler et al. 1999). The idea behind this is that branding is much more effective if it is targeted at what stakeholders want. Here, branding is not only about sending messages but also about receiving messages.

The idea is to understand stakeholders' concerns and wishes and to design a brand that reflects these (cf. Lees-Marshment 2004); it is about developing a brand that is a response to stakeholders' demands. It is about responsiveness more than persuasion. Note that interactive approaches can still be rather one-sided if they are carried out as a form of superficial consultation rather than intense interaction with citizens or consumers. Within interactive branding approaches, parties may respond to voters by looking at polls or voters' opinion surveys and then adapt the brand. In that case, stakeholders are not actively involved in the brand making, but the brand maker responds to what he sees to be the voters' concerns and political opinions. It is also possible, however, to construct brands together with stakeholders, as we shall see in Chapter 4.

The Possibility of Counter Branding

Notwithstanding efforts by governments to manage branding processes, they cannot enforce uniformity of meaning among stakeholders. An essential feature of governance processes is that governmental agencies cannot control or impose problem definitions and often also solutions on other stakeholders, and this essential character will not change when branding is used. In governance processes, it is possible for some form of counter branding to emerge.

Counter branding can of course also be observed in the case of private brands (see Klein 2000). Interestingly, this probably happens most in cases where public values are at stake in the brand. Contestation of private brands is usually not about whether the soap cleans properly, but whether it is environmental friendly, produced in a carbon neutral way, free from child labor, and so forth. One can think of the many attempts to give new meaning to

Figure 2.2 BP original logo and an altered logo.

the BP brand after the large oil spill that caused significant environmental and economic damage in the Gulf of Mexico in 2010. One of the counter-branding activities was a contest to adapt the BP logo (see Figure 2.2).

So, the contestation of brands revolves mainly around public values that may be at stake. In governance processes, there are always public values at stake.

Figure 2.3   Photos of George W. Bush used by the White House (top left) and critics (top right and bottom).

Even more so, public values are usually at the heart of governance processes. In most governance processes, actors struggle about which values are at stake, for example environmental values, economic values, or social values. Thus we may expect multiple interpretations and contestation of brands to be even more intense in governance processes than in private branding processes.

Examples of counter-branding activities can be found in the case of the George W. Bush brand. The former American president's administration tried to brand Bush as a leader of the nation. The most important associations that were actively branded with his name and appearance were decisiveness, leader in the fight against terrorism, and military leader. The carefully managed event where Bush landed on an aircraft carrier and stepped out of a jet in military uniform to announce that the mission in Iraq was accomplished was one of the many ways in which attempts were made to create the association of strong leadership (see also Box 3.1 and Figure 6.3). However, in popular culture he was often branded as somebody who was not so clever and as somebody who had a lot in common with monkeys (see the pictures in Figure 2.3).

Especially towards the end of Bush's presidential period, the counter brands were often more effective than the brand. The George W. Bush example illustrates how multiple actors can launch campaigns to brand somebody or something. Therefore, the meaning of a brand can often not be controlled by the authorities. In governance processes, one must be aware of attempts at counter branding or attempts to damage or challenge the brands that are created in those processes. And, to fully understand brands and their working in governance processes, it is just as important to analyze these attempts as the attempts to create the brand in the first place.

2.7   CONCLUSION: THE ADDED VALUE OF THE BRANDING PERSPECTIVE

We have seen in this chapter that there is a wide variety of forms of branding both in the private sphere and in the public sphere. We have argued that the branding perspective adds something essential to public administration perspectives that so far has been largely ignored, that is, the role of influencing perceptions and motivating actors by means of symbolic constructions that mainly work by means of associations and emotions. This distinguishes branding from, for instance, the well-known perspective of framing that focuses more on argumentation processes and constructing rational and logical arguments.

In the next chapters, we elaborate how this is achieved and what branding can contribute to governance processes. We shall see how branding is used to influence perceptions about policy problems and solutions in governance processes (Chapter 3), how it contributes to activate and bind actors to these processes (Chapter 4), and how branding is used to cope with media attention (Chapter 5).

3   Branding to Influence Perceptions about Policy Problems and Solutions

3.1 INTRODUCTION

In 2002, a major political change took place in Rotterdam when a new party called Leefbaar Rotterdam (led by Pim Fortuyn[1]) became the biggest political party. They formed a coalition government with the Christian Democrats and introduced new policies on immigration and housing in districts with major socio-economic problems. The new coalition defined the continuous influx of people with low incomes, often immigrants, as a major problem for such districts. From the start it was clear that, although the discussion was about low-income groups as a whole, the immigrant aspect was very important.

The policies gave rise to many protests. The municipality was accused of introducing policies that were extremely harsh and tough on immigrants. Opponents of the ban on low-income people taking up residence in these districts argued that it caused discrimination and that it was against general laws of equal treatment. The municipality countered the critique by explaining their policies and branding them as the "Rotterdam Approach." By branding their approach in this way and distinguishing it from other approaches, they did at least three things at the same time. Firstly, they communicated that this idea came from Rotterdam and that it was something to be proud of. The municipality communicated feelings of *pride and courage* not only by explicitly naming their policies the Rotterdam Approach but also by stressing that they were the first city in the country to really face problems and deal with them. The municipality explained that the problem in the districts was the high number of people with low incomes and socio-economic problems, especially immigrants. The solution was therefore no longer to accept people with low incomes. Secondly, with the brand they communicated and symbolized the strong points of their policy approach. The municipality stressed that their policies were for the good of the people in backward neighborhoods that were already suffering from high numbers of people with low incomes, especially immigrants (see also Bol and de Langen 2006). They communicated *attentiveness* as opposed to neglect by former leaders and their policies. They presented their policies as a radical break with former policies and distinguished them clearly from the policies of the past. Thirdly, through the brand, the municipality stressed aspects not only of policy content, but also of policy style and attitude. They branded the Rotterdam Approach with associations such as anti-bureaucracy, no-nonsense, and straightforwardness. This helped to distinguish the policies from intellectual ideas that do not work in practice and added feelings of familiarity with, and appreciation of, the common people as opposed to intellectuals.

Branding as Constructing Policy Content and Influencing Perceptions

The example shows how both the content and style of policies are branded. In their branding of the Rotterdam Approach, the municipality reconstructed the policy content, especially the policy problem (the presence of too many people with low incomes, especially immigrants, in a number of districts). They also singled out the policy solution, namely, banning people with low incomes, especially immigrants, from taking up residence in these districts.

In a way, the branding of the Rotterdam Approach is comparable to what Labour in Britain did with their "New Labour" and the "Third Way" examples described in Chapters 1 and 2, in that the brands influence perceptions of policy content by singling out certain characteristics of social problems and labeling them as policy problems.

Branding as an Alternative Strategy for Influencing Perceptions

Thus, brands can reconstruct policy problems and connect them to certain policy solutions—one of the core aspects of the struggle around policy content in governance processes (Koppenjan and Klijn 2004); but brands do so in a different way than other approaches in public administration, as we argue in this chapter. Brands influence actors' perceptions and problem definitions by presenting images, associations, and emotions. This is different from most other governance perspectives, which emphasize deliberative processes and argumentation and rarely address the emotional and image dimension of influencing perceptions. We think that this is an omission, because emotions are crucial in the relationships in governance networks. Also, emotions play an important role in the struggles around values that commonly take place in governance processes when actors have different views on policy problems and solutions.

This chapter draws on the literature from public administration and policy sciences, as well as the literature on marketing and branding, to understand branding as a strategy for influencing perceptions of policy content in governance processes. In section 3.2, we explore the development of policy content in governance processes by focusing on the construction of policy problems and solutions. In section 3.3, we deal with the issue of influencing perceptions in governance through instrumental approaches (aiming to influence perceptions in a predefined direction determined by a managing actor) and through interactive approaches (aiming to organize processes of interaction in which actors develop new perceptions). In sections 3.4 and 3.5, we shift the focus to branding as a process for giving meaning to policy content: in section 3.4 we explore instrumental forms of branding, and section 3.5 subsequently deals with the influencing of perceptions through interactive branding processes. We draw conclusions in section 3.6.

3.2 GOVERNANCE AND POLICY CONTENT: DEFINING POLICY PROBLEMS AND SOLUTIONS

Defining and constructing policy problems or social problems is recognized in much of the governance literature as one of the key aspects of governance processes. After all, government action is required only if a situation is recognized as a problem. But problems are not as straightforward as they seem. As Edelman (1988, 18) says: "Because a social problem is not a verifiable entity but a construction that furthers ideological interests, its explanation is bound to be part of the process of construction rather than a set of falsifiable propositions." This already indicates that assessing the nature of the policy problem is far from easy, for three reasons: policy problems are not objective entities as Edelman's remark shows; they involve political struggles; and they are dynamic. We have to look at these characteristics first to appreciate the role of branding in framing and reframing policy problems.

The Social Constructive Character of Policy Problems

If there is one thing on which scholars in public administration agree, it is the idea that (policy) problems are social constructions. As Dery (2000, 40) puts it, "[P]roblems do not exist 'out there'." Rather, they are constructed by actors in a process of *problem definition*. This becomes clear if we look at most definitions of (policy) problems: the gap between an actual situation and a desired situation (Dery 1984). Altogether, a problem consists of three elements: (1) a desirable standard; (2) a condition or situation; and (3) a connection between the standard and the situation constructed as a gap that should not exist (Hoppe 2002).

Actors' problem definitions thus depend on their perceptions of the conditions, but even more on their perception of the desirable standard. After all, the nature and urgency of the problem depend on the difference between the standard and the perceived current conditions. That means that problem definitions are based on frames of reference and values that actors hold, and these may differ fundamentally from each other. There is no possible way to define a problem without drawing on a particular frame of reference or set of values, and therefore it is impossible to define problems objectively, that is, without being colored by a frame (see also section 2.4; Koppenjan and Klijn 2004; Schön and Rein 1994). Nevertheless, actors involved in governance processes in practice often treat problem definitions as if they are objectively the best problem definition, especially if there is consensus about that problem definition.

This also means that problems are not necessarily the same as situations that hurt people. As Edelman (1988, 13) remarks, a bit cynically maybe, but correctly: "The impoverishment and massacre of a high proportion of the American Indian population was not a problem while it was happening, but only became one after it was a fait accompli." Thus (policy) problems are human constructions depending on value judgments in specific contexts such as a specific time period or a specific social group. This is crucial, because that makes them subject to change and something that can be altered by changing perceptions, introducing new standards, and creating new images. The process of policy definition and framing is essential to create support for certain governmental actions and to mobilize resources. After all, why bother if a condition is not seen as problematic?

So far, we have dealt with processes of defining a condition as a problem, but this is only a first step in governance processes. Not all problems become *policy* problems. This is important, because one aspect of branding policy content is about branding problems in such a way that they become perceived as policy problems.

Two conditions enhance the chances of problems entering the policy agenda and becoming policy problems. Firstly, actors need to believe that something should be done about a problem (Kingdon 1984), in particular by policymakers. Therefore the problem should be considered severe enough. Problems need to be worth solving (Wildavsky 1979). Secondly, problem definitions are more likely to reach the policy agenda when they carry "opportunities for improvement" (Dery 2000, 40). Dery (2000) points out that one of the criteria for problems to become policy problems is the criterion of feasibility. This can be explained as follows: people are more likely to acknowledge the existence of a problem once they think they can actually do something about it. Edelman even argues that policy solutions come before policy problems, in both a chronological and psychological sense (Edelman 1988).[2] Nonetheless, it must be noted that some problems are on the policy agenda long before solutions are in sight (see e.g. Kingdon 1984). Not all problems are acknowledged only after a solution has appeared, although the appearance of a solution may enhance the acknowledgment of a problem.

In summary, two things enhance the chances of a problem becoming a policy problem: actors in a governance network need to have the perception that something should be done, and they need to feel that something can be done; and that makes branding and brands interesting because brands often do just that: create images and associations that not only catch people's attention but also create feelings of desire for something and evoke images of desirable solutions. Of course creating the feeling among large groups of stakeholders that a certain problem is worth solving and that certain solutions are desirable is quite different than creating the feeling of being attractive and sexy because of using a certain perfume, but the important resemblance is that they both create images of desirable solutions to human problems.

Defining Policy Problems and Solutions Involves Political Struggles

The development of policy content is also a political process. How policy content is defined in terms of particular problems and certain solutions is directly related to which issues attract political attention and how public money is spent. Kingdon (1984, 11) explains: "Some are helped and others are hurt, depending on how problems get defined. If things are going basically your way, for instance, you want to convince others that there are no problems out there." And Cobb and Elder (1983, 110) argue in their well-known book about agenda setting: "The greater the size of the audience to which an issue can be enlarged, the greater the likelihood that it will attain systemic agenda standing and thus access to a formal agenda."

Thus, problem definitions are inherently political. They are tied to processes of creating support, constructing attractive images, and people that benefit from solving the problem. Those processes need associations, images, and story lines that stick with the wider public. Stone contends that problem definition is political by arguing that it is a matter of image making, whereby she stresses aspects of attributing cause, blame, and responsibility. Actors deliberately portray problems "in ways calculated to gain support for their side" (Stone 1989, 282). Policy problems, therefore, are not only about constructing a problem but also about reaching a wider public and political support.

The same holds for policy solutions. Edelman (1988, 24) highlights the politics behind the construction of policy *solutions*: "There are always people who benefit, or think they do, from a widespread belief that a problem has been solved or that there has been substantial progress toward its solution. When the number of such people is large or they occupy strategic positions, a regime has a strong incentive to depict as a solution any development that is associated with the problem linguistically, logically, or in fantasy." Therefore, politicians, managers, stakeholders, and other groups often construct a relation between acute policy problems and solutions and try to change those constructions when political and societal contexts change. A new highway that is presented as a solution to a traffic problem at one point in time can also be constructed as a solution to decreasing employment and economic activities in times of economic crisis. Thus the way policy problems and solutions are framed and connected to each other is dependent not only on the political process in which they take place but also on the wider political context. In that context, actions are justified as a solution for a specific problem (Dery 2000). The—often contested—construction of policy content is also related to the need of political leaders to distinguish themselves from others and to get elected. For many political leaders, this is a reason to resort to branding. Brands single out specific characteristics and associations of a good, a service, or a specific idea. Political leaders use them to connect themselves to certain combinations of problems and solutions that might be attractive to voters. The Rotterdam Approach, just like Labour's Third Way in Britain, singles out certain problems and couples them to specific actions and solutions. Branding is thus used as a strategy for distinguishing political leaders and attracting voters amidst political struggle.

Policy Content Changes over Time: The Dynamics of Problems and Solutions

If policy problems and solutions are, therefore, human constructions, they are also shaped and reshaped in interaction between people. Put differently, policy problems are formed during the complex interactions in governance networks (Dery 1984; Koppenjan and Klijn 2004). As Dery (1984) and Weiss (1989) have argued, various actors attempt to reformulate problem definitions during the decision-making process. This means that policy problems will shift over time, as will the connections between problems and solutions. Some points in time may be favorable for certain solutions, whereas that momentum may have disappeared at other times (see Kingdon 1984), and political leaders and others will also try to push their definition of the problem and make use of changes over time to shift the balance.

This may be informed by combinations of changing conditions in society or in natural systems (for example global warming), political ideology, or triggering events that have a significant impact on the way people in society see problems (see Box 3.1). In that sense, governance networks are complex systems that sometimes display high dynamics that are very difficult to predict (Gerrits 2008; Teisman et al. 2009). Thus policy problems are shaped and reshaped over time. This reflects not only political struggle but also the *Zeitgeist* (the "spirit" of the times) and the societal events in which they are shaped. Branding is applied to strategically act upon those changes and connect the ongoing changes to political leaders and their policies in ways that benefit those leaders.

Box 3.1   Branding Problems and Solutions: George W. Bush, 9/11, and the Iraq War

The terrorist attacks on the Twin Towers in New York and other American targets on 11 September 2001 had a huge impact on the way radical Islamic groups were viewed, and on the way at least the US viewed the

continued

terrorist problem and the solutions to that problem. Suddenly, far more drastic means were considered legitimate to fight enemies of the US than before 9/11. President George W. Bush reacted to the event by changing the direction of his military and foreign policies; he launched the war on terror and invaded Iraq. He drew on the attacks to rebrand his leadership; he positioned himself as a strong and determined leader, in combination with a stronger emphasis on military leadership. The icon of that branding process was probably the image of Bush emerging in May 2003 from the cockpit of a jetfighter airplane on the deck of the aircraft carrier USS Abraham Lincoln (see Bennett 2009; Lees-Marshment 2009). He was in battle dress with his helmet under his arm (see Figures 3.1 and 3.2), announcing victory in the war against Iraq. Interestingly enough, this event is exactly what branding is about. The event presents Bush as a strong military leader and commander in chief, leading the war on terrorism. The brand is not based on information or logical arguments but on creating associations with the image and the guiding slogans and speeches. The whole appearance (aircraft carrier, military uniform) was intended to create the associations of force, military power, and strength. The image was enhanced by an emotional speech constructing the military state of affairs in Iraq as a victory over Iraq and connecting them with the terrorist attacks of 9/11. It presents the military actions in Iraq as a solution to problems with terrorist attacks in the United States. The event was successful in the sense that almost all the US newspapers and major television channels (as well as many other global media) covered the event in the way intended by the Bush advisors (see Bennett 2009). From a rational point of view, one could certainly question all these associations. For instance, there was no proven relation between Iraq and the terrorist attacks in the US. Even back in 2003 a lot of people doubted the relation between Al-Qaeda and the Iraq regime of Saddam Hussein. Neither is the association of Bush as military leader based on solid facts since his military career was not very impressive. The example also shows how brands may become less successful over time. In Bush's second term as president, when the actual problems in Iraq became clear and the victory that was claimed in 2003 proved to be a bit premature, the new political reality changed the view on his policies. The Bush brand, strongly connected to the war on terror and the Iraq invasion, was severely damaged.

Weick (1979) argued that goals are not constructed prior to action, but that in fact they are created to give meaning to joint actions and combined resources that emerge. Thus meaning and goals are not the predetermined guidelines for our rational actions but created and "enacted" upon by actors just as much as they are created by managers in rational strategy-making processes as argued in the management literature (Weick 1979).

Figure 3.1   The landing of George W. Bush on the aircraft carrier USS *Abraham Lincoln.*

This insight is also very important for branding in governance processes because, even more than in private branding, actors may try to bestow new meaning upon a brand after the brand has been created. In our theorizing on branding in governance processes, we need to take into account that deliberate branding efforts will encounter continuous processes of meaning-making that make brands dynamic.

In summary, we have argued that (policy) problems are constructions and that the construction process is both political by nature and characterized by dynamics. Policy problems change over time as political leaders, managers, or interested stakeholders try to reformulate problems or their connected solutions. As we elaborate upon later in this chapter, branding can play an important role in reconstructing policy problems and solutions, and influencing perceptions of policy content. In the next section, we take the issue of influencing perceptions further by discussing two main approaches to influencing perceptions in governance processes.

3.3   INSTRUMENTAL AND INTERACTIVE APPROACHES TO INFLUENCING PERCEPTIONS

Since the construction of policy content is a crucial feature in governance, it is not surprising that public managers attempt to manage the construction of policy content and influence perceptions of policy

Table 3.1   Characteristics of Instrumental and Interactive Approaches to Influencing Perceptions of Policy Content

	Instrumental Approaches	Interactive Approaches
Goal	Policy acceptance and compliance	Overcoming ambiguity and controversy by jointly reframing problems and solutions
Mode of communication	Sending messages	Interactive deliberation
Mode of governing	Vertical	Horizontal
Assumptions about definitions of problems and solutions	Clear and fixed	Ambiguous and changing

problems and solutions. Before we deal further with the way in which brands are applied to influence perceptions in sections 3.4 and 3.5, we discuss some basic aspects of influencing perceptions in governance. We distinguish two approaches to influencing perceptions of policy content: an instrumental and an interactive approach (Termeer and Koppenjan 1997; Van Woerkum and Van Meegeren 1999; Leeuwis 2004). As we shall show, the two approaches make different assumptions about influencing perceptions and also imply different ways of achieving changes in perceptions about policy content. Table 3.1 summarizes some of the main differences between instrumental and interactive approaches to influencing perceptions.

Instrumental Approaches to Influencing Perceptions

Instrumental approaches are mostly used in top-down planning processes where problems have been defined clearly and goals have been set by an actor who is in charge. The policy content is predefined. The steering actor knows what the problem is and what the solutions are, and he wants to persuade other parties. He tries to influence their perceptions in his, predefined, direction. The main aim is usually to increase policy acceptance and compliance.

Instrumental forms of influencing perceptions often come close to persuasive communication. The general idea is to provide reasoned opinions that will convince actors and trigger voluntary changes of perceptions, attitudes, and behavior on the basis of internal motivation (see e.g. Van Woerkum and Van Meegeren 1999; Leeuwis 2004). This approach is strongly based on the conviction that existing perceptions of actors can be influenced by explicit, directed communications.

This instrumental form of influencing perceptions is typified by the Decide-Announce-Defend model, which works roughly through the following sequence:

- Decide. A select group of actors takes a decision on the basis of the information available to them. This group is hierarchically positioned above other actors, and it has the authority to take decisions. It may consist of for example political executives or experts.
- Announce. After the decision has been taken, it is announced to the outside world. The communication process with stakeholders starts after the decision has been taken.
- Defend. The decision is defended against opponents among the stakeholders.

The central aim of communication through the Decide-Announce-Defend model is to inform stakeholders that a particular decision has been taken and will be implemented, and persuade them of the rightness of the decision.

As policy instruments, instrumental forms of influencing perceptions differ clearly from regulation, which induces behavioral change through coercion or economic incentives (subsidies). Coercion does not try to change perceptions, but merely to stop behavior that is considered undesirable or unacceptable. Environmental regulations may cause a dairy farmer to stop spreading manure on his fields in winter, even when the farmer is not convinced that this will help the environment. Instrumental forms of influencing perceptions would aim to provide convincing information, for example about nitrogen emissions from manure in winter, to motivate the farmer to stop doing so. As a matter of fact, this would still be a very rational communication strategy. Branding would probably be based on different ways of communicating the message, for example using strong images of pollution and trying to associate the favored behavior with positive associations such as saving money by not wasting nutrients, or the know-how of farmers who apply manure in those periods when the land profits most from it.

Interactive Approaches to Influencing Perceptions

Instrumental approaches to changing perceptions may be less suitable for governance situations because governance is often characterized by ambiguity or controversy about policies. Actors may hold fundamentally different perceptions about what the policy problem is and what the goals should be. In such cases, trying to communicate one single content from a specific viewpoint is likely to meet resistance and reinforce fixation of perceptions (Fischer 2003). In such situations, a more interactive approach may be better. Contrary to instrumental approaches, where perceptions are influenced by one single sender, interactive approaches to influencing perceptions focus on facilitating processes in which actors can interactively construct and reconstruct perceptions. The general idea is to overcome ambiguities or controversies by reflecting on the situation at hand and developing an understanding of each other's interests and perceptions. This often involves parties putting problems into a wider perspective and distancing themselves to a certain extent from their own perspective. Therefore, more emphasis is laid on the process of constructing perceptions. Instead of convincing the involved actors of one problem definition or policy content, interactive approaches focus on enhancing communication between actors to achieve jointly accepted policy contents or at least some convergence of perceptions (see Fischer 2003; Schön and Rein 1994; Koppenjan and Klijn 2004). A typical interactive approach would include:

- making existing perceptions explicit by verbal discussion among actors;
- facilitating reflections on the perceptions and discussions among actors, and exploring similarities and dissimilarities;
- stimulating existing and new relations between involved actors and developing new perspectives to form the basis of joint action and joint problem solving.

Thus, interactive approaches work through a process of explicating perceptions, having discussions about different perceptions, and reconstructing perceptions after that. Interaction and dialogue between the various actors are a crucial precondition to achieving that, as is open access to the process (see Fischer 2003). The aim of these interactive approaches is to change the perceptions on problems and solutions and also achieve new solutions to problems.

Of course it is not always easy to attain the required process, especially when deadlocks emerge in which actors are reluctant to reflect on their perceptions (see Van Eeten 1999). Interactive processes of perception reflection may also lead to modest changes in perceptions when actors develop solutions in the form of a package deal that contains enough attractive elements for all actors to support it. In this case, it often happens that actors accept the solution (the package deal) without changing their perceptions about underlying problems.

Instrumental Approaches, Interactive Approaches, and Branding

There are significant differences between instrumental approaches and interactive approaches. Whereas instrumental approaches start from a given communication content, interactive approaches aim just to create or re-create that policy content. We wish to underline how important it is to realize that, in practice, some strategies to influence perceptions show elements of both instrumental and interactive approaches. These strategies lie somewhere on the continuum between, on the one hand, influencing perceptions in an extremely instrumental way and, on the other hand, influencing perceptions in an extremely interactive way. For example, the marketing approach to influence perceptions of political parties described by Lees-Marshment (2009) is not entirely instrumental, but it is not very interactive either. In the marketing approach that Lees-Marshment describes, political parties undertake market analysis, for example by conducting a survey, to discover what voters want. They subsequently take the ideas of voters into account in the development of their party program and the party brand. The degree to which the content of the party program is predetermined or defined in interaction with the voters determines whether the approach is more instrumental or more interactive.

The continuum from instrumental to interactive approaches to influencing perceptions can also be recognized in the literature on branding, as we explicate in the next two sections. In doing so, we wish to stress that branding approaches, whether instrumental or interactive, differ from the interactive and instrumental approaches in policy science and communication theory, which tend to emphasize the logical or at least reasonable character of the process. These approaches tend to stress either the rational construction of policy theories, or the reasonable, discursive character of the argumentative debate between actors. They are about learning processes, exploring information, constructing arguments. Brands and branding are less geared towards the rational dimension of interaction processes. They process messages via the heuristic route towards persuasion, whereas policy and communication approaches are more aimed at processing messages via the systemic route (see Box 2.1 in Chapter 2). Thus branding tries to influence perceptions in a slightly more indirect way, focusing on creating associations and emotions instead of relying on rational information, argumentation, and deliberation.

In the next sections, we explore how branding in an instrumental and interactive way works and how each would fit in governance processes.

3.4   INSTRUMENTAL BRANDING OF POLICY CONTENT: SELLING THE MESSAGE

When public managers apply branding in an instrumental way to give their meaning to policies, they create a brand as a symbol to communicate those policies. The brand is used as a symbol that presents the policy content in a particular way. Public managers select certain aspects (the problem definition, the solution, the target groups, and so on) and construct a brand in order to communicate those aspects in a way that also evokes certain predefined feelings and emotions. The example of the Rotterdam Approach as a brand, described in section 3.1, highlighted a number of things. Apart from selecting a certain phrasing of the policy problem (the problem is the low socio-economic status of the neighborhoods and their inhabitants), the Rotterdam Approach communicated feelings of decisiveness, daring, and attentiveness to the problems of the general public. In this example of instrumental branding, the policy content was branded by consciously creating a number of associations with it. It should be noted that perceptions of the Rotterdam policies were influenced not only by the Rotterdam Approach brand but also by the brand of the major political party that developed those policies, and by the brand of the city (Rotterdam traditionally has an image of a no-nonsense "working city"). The fact that the main political party behind the brand had a populist and non-elitist image made it easier for them to position their policies as attentive to problems experienced by the general public. Also, the fact that the policies were developed in Rotterdam, the no-nonsense city, facilitated associations with "telling it like it is" and actually dealing with problems instead of talking about problems. The example shows that instrumental branding of policy content takes place through a "brandscape" wherein multiple brands exist. The perception of policy content is influenced by brands that are specifically created to brand policies, but also by other brands that are related to the policies directly or indirectly. In this way, the brands are used to influence perceptions of policy content not so much by communicating the content of the policy in detailed terms (no list of measures, budgets, and policy goals is given) as by communicating key values and the style behind the policy content.

An instrumental form of branding is for instance visible in political marketing strategies that aim to sell or market political parties. "Selling" a party, as Lees-Marshment argues, works roughly through the following sequence (Lees-Marshment 2009):

- Product design: the party designs the brand, the ideas, the logo, and the behavior that fits the brand;
- Market intelligence: the party researches voters' response to the brand, for example through surveys or focus groups;
- Communication: the brand is communicated by the entire party; this means that the political leaders, but often also others, are informed about the values behind the brand and the core messages that are to be communicated;
- Campaign: setting out the brand and marketing strategy in the run-up to the election;
- Election;
- Delivery: delivery of the product in government.

This exemplifies instrumental approaches to branding. The party determines its goals and policies, and then develops a branding campaign with a carefully constructed set of images and information to be communicated in a favorable way to the target group.

Instrumental Branding: Attracting Attention through Images and Emotions

Instrumental branding is not demand driven, since actors usually do not ask to be persuaded (cf. Leeuwis 2004). Although the construction of the brand may involve market research on what relevant actors such as stakeholders or citizens think, instrumental branding is essentially about getting a predefined message across. A major problem in this approach is that actors may not be motivated to pay attention to the message because they did not ask for it. To deal with this, the sender of a message can try to attract and increase attention via peripheral cues such as affect. As explained in Box 2.1 in Chapter 2, these cues can be processed by the target group even when attention is low. This is why branding draws on emotions and images to influence perceptions. Branding is a strategy that puts more stress on peripheral cues than traditional forms of communication applied in governance processes.

Influencing Perceptions about Policy Content through Emotions

Brands connect associations to specific policy content and also try to evoke emotions that help to create and strengthen these associations. This is not surprising, since policymaking is also about winning the hearts and minds of stakeholders and the wider public. If we return to the example presented in Box 3.1—George W. Bush descending on the aircraft carrier in military uniform—we can already see this. The Bush administration not only instrumentally used this image to create associations useful for constructing the policy problem and solution (the problem is that international terrorism is a safety threat for the US homeland; the solution is military force) but also tried to evoke emotions. The leader and his policies were explicitly connected to a victory, triggering emotions that arise on winning a difficult battle and celebrating victory: jubilant feelings, as well as emotions of joy and delight. The spectacular event of the president landing on an aircraft carrier on the high seas furthered the excitement and thrill.

The event also drew on the inclinations and wishes of people to belong to the winning party; this helps to bind people to the winning political leader and support his policy, his solutions, and his problem definition. Another example of instrumentally drawing on emotions comes from the electoral campaign in the US of the Republican Ronald Reagan who defeated the incumbent Democratic President Carter. According to most analysts, the fact that during the elections US citizens were taken hostage by Iranian religious republicans implicitly sent the daily message that Carter could not solve this problem. The "shame" of the US being held hostage by a relatively small country such as Iran was an important factor in Carter's defeat. Ronald Reagan effectively connected the image of "weakness" and "shame" to Carter's policies in order to position himself as a strong leader who would solve the problem. Reagan did so successfully, since the image was confirmed continuously by the media (Bennett 2009).

Thus, creating emotional associations helps to communicate substantial policy ideas and get the message across. The idea behind influencing perceptions about policy content at an emotional level is that it is at this level that people judge issues, connect to issues, and become motivated to give attention to the policy problem (see e.g. Batey 2008; Marcus 2000). Emotions have a strong impact on what we perceive as policy problems and solutions, on how we perceive them, and on our willingness to engage and pay attention. Emotional triggers can help to create the feeling that problems can and should be solved. Creating the idea that problems should be solved and can be solved is crucial for turning problems into policy problems (see e.g. Kingdon 1984; Dery 1984; see also section 3.2). Emotions therefore create something important that is often underestimated in public administration literature on policy problems: the motivation of actors to do something about a particular condition that is constructed as a policy problem. Consequently, it is not surprising that many politicians use emotions in their speeches and create brands of themselves and their policies to create urgency and support.

Influencing Perceptions of Policy Content through Visual Images

One picture often says more than a thousand words. This is the adage behind the use of visual techniques to influence perceptions in instrumental branding of policy content. The use of visual images in governance processes may not be as sophisticated or as widespread as it is in private sector branding. A common branding activity in policies and projects in the public sector is naming, but the names of policies and projects are only rarely integrated in visual designs through for example wordmarks or lettermarks. Also the use of visual brand elements such as pictorials and emblems is more limited than in the private sector (for examples of visual brand elements in the private sector, see Wheeler 2009). However in political life, for example, the instrumental use of the visual has become quite familiar. We already gave examples of logos and visually designed taglines in political campaigns in Chapters 1 and 2. We have also reflected extensively on the image of George W. Bush as commander. Political life nowadays is a media life, and reaching audiences through media such as television and the Internet requires visual images. We deal with this more extensively in Chapter 5 where we discuss the media and the role of branding in governance processes to cope with media attention, but for now it is important to stress that visual images can create associations much faster than texts can. Visual images are firstly communicated in photos. Text has become less dominant in many policy documents, and visual images have become more important. Urban and rural policy programs are peppered with big and colorful photos of happy people or landscapes. The photos are not meant to communicate the policy content directly; rather, they are inserted mainly to communicate a certain feeling and atmosphere that the policy-makers want to connect to their policies, for example happiness, success, or joy. Thus, a policy document on revitalization may show diverse groups of happy people in their (sunny) neighborhood. Pictures of joyful children, for example, may be used to trigger warm feelings and communicate in yet another way why the revitalization is so important.

In addition to photographic material, images in policy documents also come in the shape of graphs and maps in which the use of color is an important aspect in branding policy content. Colors are used to influence ideas about what the problems are. In tables and figures, the color red is often used to signal "problem," whereas the color green is often used to signal "going well." By coloring a particular geographical area in red, the area is branded as a problem area. In a table, one can depict a declining population in "red" in order to enhance the impression of a problem.

Besides visuals in documents, iconic architecture is used to visualize and communicate certain aspects of governance programs. For example, the Øresund Bridge, as discussed in Chapter 2, was used to construct the policies of the governments involved as connecting countries. The Eiffel Tower in Paris visualizes French progress and success. The Guggenheim in Bilbao constructs the city's urban policies as friendly to the arts and the creative class. The icon thus not only draws attention to the city, but also communicates something substantial about the city and its policies.

Limitations of Instrumental Branding: Contestation and Varying Perceptions

Instrumental branding is a form of branding whereby a manager or elected officeholder tries to communicate a predefined message. Given the character of governance processes, this approach by definition has its limitations. Instrumental approaches implicitly assume that one message can be communicated and that, at least to a certain extent, one can control the associations that are constructed around the brand. Now, this assumption has already proven to be invalid for several private brands. There are many examples where constructed brands did not have the intended effect on consumers, or where brands were confronted with attempts to damage the brand (see e.g. Loken and Roedder John 2010). This may be even stronger in governance processes, since these are characterized by multiple actors with different or even conflicting interests, and various perceptions of the problem. These actors will almost always give different meanings to the brand. Thus, the ways created brands are experienced and reconstructed by the involved actors may differ considerably. This means that created brands are subject to reinterpretations. They may assume a different meaning than that intended by the creator. Box 3.2 gives an example of varying interpretations of a community brand.

Box 3.2   Experiencing a Community Brand in Different Ways

The Witte de With neighborhood near the center of Rotterdam deteriorated in the 1970s and '80s. At the beginning of the 1990s, local government tried to improve the neighborhood. An important part of the improvement process was an attempt to give the neighborhood a new image and to brand it as cultural and exciting (the neighborhood is close to several museums). In policy documents, by subsidizing cultural events, and by using free publicity in media (for instance local newspapers), local government tried to rebrand the neighborhood as cultural, creative, and inspiring; but at the same time the neighborhood already had many bars and restaurants. That part was not actively branded by officials. Stok et al. (2008) undertook research in which they confronted a number of residents (50), owners of shops and bars (13), and policymakers (13) with a number of images of their neighborhood. It turned out that different groups gave different slants when they were asked to react to a number of statements about the neighborhood. Respondents interpreted the neighborhood brand differently than the municipality had meant it. Whereas the municipality wanted to brand the neighborhood as cultural and creative, the majority of respondents perceived it mainly as cozy and lively with many bars and restaurants. When asked to characterize the neighborhood in three words, respondents' dominant terms were "cozy" and "village in the city." This was especially the case with residents and the owners of shops and bars. Policymakers more often mentioned characteristics of the official brand relating to a cultural neighborhood. This can also be seen in Figure 3.2, presenting the three groups of respondents and their answer to the question as to how important bars and restaurants are for the image of the neighborhood (1 = very important; 5 = very unimportant). This highlights the fact that brands can be created but: (1) brands co-evolve with the existing perceptions and the situation in the neighborhood where bars and restaurants are fairly dominant; (2) brands are subject to (re)interpretation by various actors who not only understand the brand in their own way and re-create the brand accordingly, but also may have conflicting or different views on the brand.

Besides the normal differences in interpretation of brands, brands can be contested. This is also known from private branding practices since the Internet contains lots of small video clips in which existing well-known brands are mocked or even damaged (see also Loken and Roedder John 2010). This means that analyzing brands also involves analyzing the various perceptions of the involved actors (see Koppenjan and Klijn 2004) to understand how the brand fits with the different perceptions of the actors and what the effect of that might be.

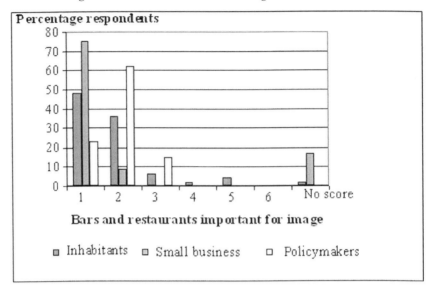

Figure 3.2 Importance of catering industry for the image of the neighborhood.

Thus, although the content of a message is predefined, it may become contested or even counter branded at several points. Firstly, it may be contested within government offices or within a network of core stakeholders before it is communicated to the public; secondly, it may be contested after the message has been communicated to the public. Consequently, maybe even more than in private settings, branding in governance needs careful analysis if it is to have the intended effect on perceptions of policy content. To be able to make reasonable statements about the effects of brands, we need to research the perceptions of the different stakeholders and the opinions of the wider public and thereby, importantly, take into account the dynamics in meaning-making to which brands are subject.

Dynamics in Instrumental Branding

As already stated, meaning-making in governance processes is a dynamic process. The branding of policy content is also a form of meaning-making, and it is not free of dynamics as we have argued in the previous section. Dynamics in the meaning of a brand may result from contestation of the brand by stakeholders, but may also result from slowly occurring changes in perception. The public may start to perceive a brand differently over time. For example, the George W. Bush brand came to be interpreted very negatively towards the end of his presidency—an interpretation that differed markedly from that in vogue just after the terrorist attacks on 9/11 when he was seen as a strong leader who took the nation by the hand.

However, brands may also change due to more consciously managed changes that brand owners try to bring about, for example attempts to extend the brand. There are several reasons why public managers may try to change the meaning of a brand. An obvious reason is that politicians have changed the course of their policies and want the brand to adapt accordingly. Another reason is that brands tend to wear out (see e.g. Tellis 2004), and especially in the public sector so it seems. People regularly become disillusioned by policies and their brands and so public brands need a new impetus now and then.

What is important when it comes to changing the meaning of brands is to find a balance between continuity and change. If a brand changes too often, citizens may get the feeling that the brand could mean anything. The brand starts to lose meaning and credibility. However, if the meaning of the brand is not being adapted to emerging preferences of citizens, the popularity of the brand may decrease. As described in Chapters 1 and 2, Tony Blair and his Labour Party adapted the meaning of the Third Way brand slightly by introducing partnerships as a central policy idea. The introduction of new policy ideas can rejuvenate public brands.

3.5 INTERACTIVE BRANDING: A PROCESS OF JOINT DEVELOPMENT OF POLICY CONTENT

Interactive branding involves a process of brand building in which actors jointly develop a brand. Contrary to instrumental branding, where the brand is mostly created by a single actor and based on market research or other information, interactive branding is a joint process where various actors contribute to the construction of the brand. The interactive process may be tightly organized in the form of a highly planned process with several facilitated interactive sessions, but it may also be less organized when a brand manager makes possible only certain events in which a community of people meets and (re)produces a community brand.

In the more planned and organized form of interactive branding, actors jointly determine what brand they want to develop and how they will brand policy content. In this interactive process, the actors usually deliberate on the branding process and the underlying policy problems and solutions. The branding process is not only used to communicate a message as in instrumental branding; it also is used to facilitate discussion about policy issues. The development of the brand is used to discuss questions such as "what is the core problem that we want to address?" and "what are the key values behind our policy?" In other words, the branding process becomes a strategy for jointly developing visions on policy problems and solutions.

The less tightly organized form of interactive branding may be compared to what happens in so-called brand communities (McAlexander et al. 2002; Muniz and O'Guinn 2001). Brand communities are communities of people who feel mutually related because of their shared interest in a particular brand, for example the Saab brand community, the Jeep brand community, or the Apple brand community (Muniz and O'Guinn 2001). Brand communities create brands in an interactive way, since they have "an active interpretive function, with brand meaning being socially negotiated, rather than delivered unaltered" (Muniz and O'Guinn 2001, 414). In the Saab brand community, for instance, owners of Saab cars meet and communicate with each other about Saab. During the meetings, they talk and tell each other stories that construct and reproduce the qualities of Saab. The characteristics of the Saab brand are being constructed and reproduced. For example, Saab owners tell each other stories about being in a car accident but coming out of it without personal injury thanks to the great safety that the car offers. These stories construct and confirm the reputation that the Saab brand has when it comes to car safety. The content of the stories cannot be managed by the brand owner, but the brand owner can facilitate and organize occasions or websites on which the community members can meet and interact. In the public sector, such brand communities may not be as clearly visible as with some private brands, but one can perceive brand communities within political parties. Political parties' brands are partly created by communication professionals, but also formed interactively within the community of party members. Strong brand communities can create feelings of "we-ness" and a common connection to the brand. This can lead to brand loyalty and commitment to the content of the brand.

This is one of the reasons why interactive branding can be important for governance processes. Since governance is characterized by multiple stakeholders, it could be very interesting to try to bind these stakeholders to a common idea inscribed in the brand. After all, stakeholder cooperation is crucial in governance processes. Thus, creating a brand together in an interactive way can enhance the support for the brand and the content it stands for.

The Openness of Brands as a Quality in Governance Processes

Brands can facilitate the development of common understanding because their meaning is not entirely fixed. Actors can develop the meaning of a brand during a process of interaction. It is the ambiguity of symbols and concepts that allows actors with different perceptions of problems and solutions to share ideas by using the same symbol while at the same time giving a (slightly) different meaning to it. Anthropological studies on the use of symbols have established that members of a community who are united through the use of particular shared symbols may give different meanings to those symbols (Cohen 1985). Similar findings have been reported in the policy analysis literature; actors may give a partly different and a partly shared meaning to broad concepts such as sustainability (Hajer 1995). The open character of brands and their sometimes slightly ambiguous character can be a quality in governance processes that are often complex and where there is a need to find innovative solutions during the process that satisfy the various actors and their different perceptions. The partly open content of brands allows for development. The meaning of brands can develop when people use them in their daily lives or other social contexts (such as governance processes). The McDonald's brand becomes filled with the meaning of joy and family during and after eating at McDonald's with the children. As Arvidsson (2006, 82) argues, "[B]rand identity is only realized insofar as consumers are involved in its co-creation. It is only when consumers let brands be part of their lives, when brands initiate 'enduring relationships' with consumers or become 'living ideas' that can transform people's lives." The Volvo brand becomes especially meaningful to a man when he can safely and comfortably transport his children in his car. The brand becomes meaningful in his relationship with his children as a caring father. As a matter of fact, the Volvo brand can also be meaningful in his relationship with neighbors, because owning a Volvo may position him in a specific way. It may establish a certain status.

The development of brand meaning is similar in governance processes. Brands acquire meaning in the process of interaction; their meaning is filled in by the involved actors and shaped by the perceptions of these actors. The case in Box 3.3 exemplifies how branding is effected in a process of mutual interaction between actors.

Box 3.3   Branding Interactive Decision-Making Processes: The Example of Zuidplaspolder

The Zuidplaspolder, an area in the west of the Netherlands between the cities Rotterdam, Gouda, and Zoetermeer, came to existence in the nineteenth century when it was drained dry. Until then, it was a polder filled with water. Until the 1960s, it was mainly an agricultural polder characterized by an open landscape with pastures. Since then, the greenhouse culture has gradually become more important, and the area has also urbanized under pressure from the expanding cities of Rotterdam and Zoetermeer.

Recently, water-management problems have becoming pressing. Discussions on global warming have resulted in the conviction that the polder needs to be prepared for handling higher quantities of water in more erratic flows. Also, changes in national water policies have fueled the idea of increasing water storage capacity. As a result, the creation of more wetlands in the Zuidplaspolder has been put on the political agenda.

At the same time, environmental groups complain about the ongoing industrial and urban activities that result in an incremental but steady loss of the green characteristics of the original polder.

Continued

In 2002, the province takes the initiative to start an interactive process to explore the possibilities for an integral development of the Zuidplaspolder.

The province tries to involve all main stakeholders from the start. A large group of 23 stakeholders is involved in the decision-making process by means of a steering committee. The actors vary from environmental groups and agricultural organizations to the municipalities in the area and several central departments (Ministry of Transport, Ministry of Housing, and Ministry of Agriculture).

The project group sets up a fairly open and interactive decision-making process. This interactive character is stressed also in a document prepared by the province (beginning of 2003), the initiator of the process. The province emphasizes the communicative and participative character of the process. Using the idea of a participation ladder, the document identifies the way of involvement and the communication activities for each target group (Van Buuren et al. 2010). The actors work on a joint area map that shows the possiblities and impossibilities for each part of the area. Directly from the beginning, the project group tries to communicate a specific image of the project. It tries to brand the project as a special project in which, in a modern and interactive way, climate-friendly solutions are combined with crucial other functions (e.g. new dwellings and greenhouses). Both the content and the process of the project are branded through the key words innovative, climate friendly, interactive, and integral development.

The communication department is an important and active part of the project group. It implements an intensive communication strategy by means of large conferences, media exposure, a newsletter, and a website. The steering committeee and the project group try to brand the project in the sense that they aim to add meaning to the project, and distinguish it from other projects. A concrete manifestation of the brand is the signature (a formally defined combination of a logotype and a brandmark) that the steering committee uses (see Figure 3.3). Another concrete brand element that is part of the branding strategy is the fixed font and color system that is used in the steering group's publications.

Although the communication strategy is not explicitly aimed at feelings or the emotional, it does communicate emotionally loaded ideas such as innovation (optimism and excitement), climate friendliness (commitment and empathy), and integrative solutions (hope). It also communicates that the whole planning process is undertaken with other stakeholders (interactive character). A brand has been developed interactively to symbolize the plans for the polder. The actors in the project group have developed and filled in the content of the brand over time.

Source: Van Buuren et al. 2010.

Figure 3.3 Signature of the steering committee of the Zuidplaspolder project.

The Usage of Brands in Management of Perceptions

Branding can therefore be useful in governance processes because it addresses an important element of governance processes: it provides the possibility to deal with perceptions of actors, especially because brands can appeal to actors with different perceptions. Brands are "unfinished" and open in the sense that their production and reproduction takes place in interaction among actors in governance processes. Brands do not force but rather seduce actors to participate in an interaction process, thus enabling them to build a kind of rough consensus about where to go. And then they can fulfill another function of governance processes discussed in Chapter 4: the binding of actors.

3.6   CONCLUSIONS

In this chapter, we have indicated that branding is a strategy for giving policies certain meanings by connecting them with meaningful symbols and images, rather than by constructing problems and solutions discursively by use of particular story lines and arguments. Branding thus differs from the discursive framing of problems and solutions. Branding policy content is built on the idea that judgment is driven by emotions (see also Chapter 2). This is why branding is aimed at "engaging the heart before the mind" (Pasotti 2010, 14).We have also shown that the meaning of brands and how brands influence perceptions of policy content are determined not only by brand owners or public managers who try to build a brand, but also by other actors in governance networks, such as citizen groups. Attempts to brand policy content in a particular way may be undertaken by public managers, but also by other actors. The brand itself may even become contested. This can make the influencing of perceptions through branding a practice that may prove to be more complex than it seems to public managers who hope for the silver bullet that will align all perceptions in a predefined way. One way of dealing with this, as described in this chapter, is interactive branding. This is about actively involving stakeholders in the creation of the brand.

For researchers, the multiplicity of interpretations of brands means that it is important to carefully analyze how branding activities and brands are perceived among multiple actors. To be able to make reasonable statements about the effects of brands, researchers need to take into account the perceptions of the different stakeholders and the opinions of the wider public.

4   Branding to Activate, Motivate, and Bind Stakeholders in Governance Processes

4.1   INTRODUCTION

The construction of the Lyon–Turin segment of the new European high speed rail network, first proposed in the 1990s, is one of the key projects in the European program called the Trans European Transport Network (TEN-T). The aim is to connect Lyon with the Ukrainian border. In 2001, the French and Italian government sign a treaty to secure the construction of the line, and in 2004 the project is confirmed by the EU as one of the most important projects in the TEN-T. In the communications about the project, it is positioned as very important for European transport and, later, as essential in reducing the number of motor vehicles, especially heavy goods vehicles, traveling through the tunnels in the Alps. In 2007, the European Union allocates 671.8 million Euros to partly fund the tunnel over the period 2007–2013.

From the start however, the project raises opposition from the people in the Susa valley in the north of Italy, through which the railway has to pass. Inhabitants protest against the high speed train system (TGV) because they fear the construction will damage health and environment in the valley (Marincioni and Appiotti 2009). In 2007, after the funding decision of the European Union, one of the spokesmen for the protesters says: "The countdown has begun. A small effort and we will have won. The TGV will not pass through the Susa valley" (http://www.cafebabel.co.uk/article/21166/lyon-turin-countdown-to-the-tgv.html). Despite extensive efforts by the Italian government to look for alternatives and provide counter arguments against the negative effects of the railway, the opposition does not cease. Analysts argue that certainly one of the problems with this project is that stakeholders were involved late. Earlier contact with stakeholders would have facilitated the development of other perceptions of risks among people living in the area, and it would have resulted in less resistance (Marincioni and Appiotti 2009).

This case exemplifies not only how prestigious projects can encounter strong resistance, but also the need to communicate and interact with stakeholders.

Brands as Creating Images and Binding Actors in Large Projects

It is therefore not surprising that public managers try to enhance support for, and commitment to, their projects and programs among a larger audience; and to do so, they must communicate the idea of the project to that audience. Some public managers have started to draw on branding techniques, for example creating icons, logos, and slogans. Branding was not really applied in the Lyon–Turin example, but other examples of cross-European projects do show clear traces of branding. One example is the Øresund Bridge, discussed in section 2.2. The bridge connects Copenhagen (Denmark) and Malmö (Sweden), and explicit attempts have been made to brand both the project and the region. The project was branded as connecting people, and the region between Copenhagen and Malmö was branded as a united entity (Hospers 2006). A specific organization called the Øresund Identity Network, which includes about 150 companies and public organizations (Hospers 2006), was created to further the branding of the region. The branding was achieved by developing a main theme that would give the region a clear profile. In addition, logos and slogans were developed (see Figure 4.1), as well as a logotype (the Ø). The region was advertised in newspapers and websites in order to increase its profile.

The aim of the Øresund branding is to connect the Danish and the Swedish communities and present the region in a more coherent way to investors and tourists. Thus its aim is not only to create a (visual) image but also to attract various kind of stakeholders to a joint activity, which in this case is the governance of the economic and social development of a region. Interestingly, the logo clearly uses the image of the Øresund Bridge to create the association of connecting and binding people. But things do not always evolve as planned, as the Lyon–Turin railway shows. Large projects often generate resistance, and then they may suddenly be presented in a quite different way than planned. Protesters try to create a completely different image of the project with entirely different associations than intended by the initiators. Counter images may be created, and in some cases protesters engage in counter branding. In the latter case, they try to change the brand and the associations that are triggered by the brand. As explained in Chapter 2, brands can be criticized or even mocked. Brands and logos therefore can also arouse negative emotions and activations.

Figure 4.1   Visual representation of the Øresund Bridge brand.

Brands as Activating and Binding Actors to Governance Networks

Thus we see how brands, including a variety of brand elements such as visual images, logos, and story lines, can raise attention and help to draw actors to a policy process, but they can also trigger the development of counter images and attract opponents. This is the subject we deal with in this chapter: how brands can contribute to activating and motivating, but also to binding, actors to governance processes. In this chapter, on the basis of marketing theory, public administration theory, and policy science theory, we discuss the mechanisms through which branding activates and binds actors. We give examples showing that the mechanisms do occur in practice and also indicating the kind of cases in which they can be found. However, we must realize, as mentioned in Chapter 1, that branding in governance processes is only in its infancy, and that we are witnessing only the start of the mechanisms described in this chapter.

In section 4.2, we discuss why activating and binding actors is so important in governance processes. In section 4.3, we take a first look at how branding can contribute to this. Section 4.4 then digs deeper into the question of how branding can activate and bind actors in complex governance processes. In section 4.5, we draw some conclusions.

4.2 MODERN GOVERNANCE AND THE NEED TO MOTIVATE AND ACTIVATE ACTORS

In modern governance processes, government does not have all the resources to develop and implement policies on its own. This means that governments try to include various stakeholders in policy initiatives. Why is this important, and what are the consequences of this stakeholder involvement?

Why Is Stakeholder Involvement Important in Governance Processes?

The governance networks that deal with complex problems are made up of sets of actors with enduring interdependencies. These networks require different decision-making procedures involving more actors at earlier stages of the policy formation process. New horizontal forms of governance aim to provide a solution to the problems that plague traditional, more top-down decision making. If we look at the main problems mentioned in the literature, we see that these can be grouped into four categories: veto players obstructing decision making; fixed problem definitions; fixed problem solutions; and democratic legitimacy (see e.g. Rhodes 1997; Kickert et al. 1997; Pierre 2000; Sørensen and Torfing 2007). Table 4.1 summarizes those problems.

The veto argument reduces to the fact that, in governance processes, governments need various actors with important resources, but these actors can block decisions. Top-down steering will not solve this problem. If governments want to restructure neighborhoods, they have to deal with actors like housing corporations who own the dwellings and various groups of citizens that can block decisions. And classical central steering creates other problems as

Table 4.1   Governance as a Solution to Steering Problems

Theme	Problem in Classical Decision Making	Governance as a Solution
Veto power	As various actors have important resources, they can block decision making for long or short periods. This is costly and causes long decision-making processes.	By involving more groups of actors, and different ones, than in traditional decision making, governance tries to increase support and diminish the use of veto powers.
Changing the problem definition	Being human constructs, problems tend to change during the course of interaction, as a result of confrontation with different perceptions, new information, or external developments. Mostly, however, the problem definition is fixed at the beginning, forming the starting point for the search for solutions.	Involving more actors introduces more variety into the problem definition, avoiding over-fixation on one aspect of the problem, and reducing the probability that the original problem definition will have to be reformulated. Also, more ideas for solutions are envisaged, so if the problem definition changes, more options are available as solutions.
Fixed solutions	As solutions are chosen at a relatively early stage, they are fixed, and subsequent negotiations on changes are difficult and costly. There is also the risk that a solution chosen at an early stage will not match the changed problem definition at a later decision-making stage.	Involving more actors and organizing more competition to come up with solutions will produce more alternative solutions, increasing the likelihood of new innovative solutions being found and solutions developed that could meet changing problem definitions.
Democratic legitimacy	As decision making is mostly rather closed to non-specialists, policy proposals tend to attract a lot of criticism from society. This lack of democratic legitimacy for decisions is aggravated by the fact that relations between political parties and citizens have diminished substantially (the invisible citizen).	Involving more actors (especially citizens' groups) enhances political legitimacy and creates a platform for interaction between politicians and citizens (the citizen becomes "visible").

well. Because there is only one initiator, a narrow definition of the problem is used, and the initiator tends to move quickly to one preferred solution, ignoring other knowledge available from other actors. If decision making takes a long time and problem definitions shift, as often happens because problem definitions are human constructions that change over time, we are left with an inadequate problem definition (because it is narrow and fixed) and inadequate solutions. Besides the arguments about vetoes and policy content (problems and solutions), the literature mentions that classical top-down decision making is often closed to non-specialists and that decisions in this sense are taken far away from the average citizen. Scholars often refer to the gap between citizens and politicians, arguing that more deliberative democratic models applied in a governance approach would be able to bridge that gap (see Sørenson and Torfing 2007; also Dryzek 2000 for deliberative democracy).

Horizontal forms of governance are an attempt to deal with these problems by another way of organizing decision making: with involvement of various actors, using broader problem definitions at the start. In that sense, they are an attempt (not necessarily successful!) to answer the problems that arise in classical decision making. An overview of the problems envisaged with classical decision making and the supposed answers provided by governance forms of steering is provided in Table 4.1.

Now the question of whether more stakeholder involvement leads to better policy outcomes is an intriguing one. There is evidence that is does. In a recent analysis based on a large number of respondents involved in environmental projects, Edelenbos et al. (2010) show that there is a positive correlation between the number of involved stakeholders and respondents' appreciation of outcomes. Further research shows that managerial effort is crucial in this success (Edelenbos and Klijn 2006; Klijn, Steijn et al. 2010). These findings match other research that stresses the importance of network management efforts (see Meier and O'Toole 2001, 2007; Mandell 2001).

Governance: Coping with Dependency and Complex Interactions

A governance approach is therefore supposed to solve some problems that appear in the more classical government approach, which tends to focus on the decisions of elected politicians and top-down processes to implement policies. But the governance approach of course also complicates the decision-making process since more actors are involved and the number of interdependencies increases.

Apart from the differences in actors' perceptions discussed in Chapter 3, the interdependencies and the complexity of decision-making processes are often mentioned as core characteristics of governance processes in networks. Interdependency is crucial for the governance network to emerge. It is interdependency that creates the necessity for actors to interact and thus engenders the governance network as a pattern of interactions. Consequently, without interdependency between the actors that need each other's resources (substantive resources like finance or authority, but also softer resources like giving or withdrawing legitimacy), governance networks would fall apart.

Governance networks manifest themselves in concrete policy interactions that we call policy games. It is possible for several games to be taking place around one policy problem (sometimes at several levels of policymaking). Complex environmental policy problems take place in networks that are composed of local, regional, and sometimes national government actors at the same time. And the interactions can take place in a complicated set of games. In the Lyon–Turin railway example, government actors are involved from various government layers (European Union, nation states, regional authorities, and municipalities), but there are also a number of other, less loosely connected, games (like EU decision-making processes, national, regional, and local decision making, in addition to complex games with semi-private and private actors). So this is truly a complicated process.

This means that governance processes take place not only in a world of interdependency but also in a world where decision-making processes are generally very complex. After all, decisions are reached in situations where we have many actors, at various positions in the network, that choose their own strategies in a complicated set of interrelated games (Koppenjan and Klijn 2004). Thus, the strategic interactions are numerous, and unforeseen events and patterns of strategic moves can happen.

Now the interdependencies mean that it is crucial to motivate, activate, and bind the actors that belong to the network in concrete policy interactions. We can identify a network of actors relevant to the restructuring of a neighborhood, but it is elementary that the important actors are actively present in the decision making about the actual restructuring. Governance processes are therefore dependent on the appropriate activation of actors (see Scharpf 1978). And after that it is crucial to *bind* actors to the policy process. After all, it is crucial that multiple actors arrive at an agreement about the content of the decisions, and this usually requires prolonged processes of negotiation. It is also important to bind actors to a network for the long term because, after a decision has been taken, implementation does not come about automatically. The actors involved in governance processes usually have to deal with setbacks and adaptations of plans; this means that they need to be committed and bound to the process over an extended period of time. Thus, activating and motivating actors in the network and binding them to the network are essential for governance to succeed; but these are no easy tasks as has been proven again and again in research and the practice of governance.

Box 4.1   Classical Ways of Communicating Policy in Administrative Life

Brands communicate images that trigger a web of associations with the target groups, whether they are consumers, clients, or citizens. This differs from the way governments used to communicate their policies in the

Continued

past. Policy documents and speeches, in which policies were explained, were the dominant way of communicating. These documents were supposed to reflect more or less rationally constructed policies. Policy documents represent a clear choice in policy goals that are translated into various policy instruments. Ideally, these documents are supported by the best theories available. The policy theory—as the set of basic assumptions on which policies have to be formulated—consists of normative theory, in addition to policy field theory, and policy instrument theory (see Klijn and Snellen 2009).

Firstly, *normative theory* establishes the normative connections between overarching value orientations, policy goals, and operational goals. In technical terms, this often translates into a hierarchical structure of goals and sub-goals (Kuijpers 1980; Dror 1968).

Secondly, *policy field theory* provides the causal chain or chains that make explicit the variables that create a policy problem in a sector of society, and the variables that politicians can choose for a more or less effective intervention in the causal chain. Research is the more or less objective basis on which policy field theory is created (Quade 1975; Hofferbert 1974; see for a criticism: Lindblom and Cohen 1979).

Thirdly, *policy instrument*, or *policy effect*, theory provides insights into which policy measures are required or most effective in achieving a certain policy goal. Policy instrument or policy effect theory relates action and sub-goals to the final goals to be achieved by a policy.

In the first place, these policy documents aimed to convince others rather than activate and bind others. The documents were part of a hierarchical form of public management, in which government decided and then tried to explain and convince others of their decision. Government did not feel very dependent on others, so activating and binding others was not their priority. Therefore, explaining and convincing was the main function of the policy documents. In the second place, these policy documents were the basis for designing incentives and instruments for changing the behavior of target groups. Policy field theory provides the policy entrepreneur with causal relations to influence by means of financial incentives (subsidies, penalties) or legal instruments (laws and regulations that prohibit certain behavior). In this classical way of communicating public policy, the rational and logical character of the message is the most important. Of course, this model has been strongly criticized since the early 1950s when Lindblom introduced his incrementalism, emphasizing that policymaking was taking small steps towards moving away from the problem and coping with insufficient information about cause and effect (Lindblom 1959; Lindblom and Cohen 1979). And many researchers have shown that actual policymaking processes are more often than not a fight between various interests and actors, and that policy documents are compromises rather than rational documents (see Cobb and Elder 1983; Kingdon 1984).

But despite all these criticisms, communicating policy was still seen as something predominantly rational, unidirectional (from government to citizens), and preferably as precisely defined and coherent as possible (clear goals and instruments). This seems not very effective in a governance context where various stakeholders have to be seduced to participate, and networks of actors have to be built and sustained. Co-production, communicating, and joint action have become more important in governance processes at the expense of implementing pre-formulated goals. Thus we see a growing tendency to communicate in ways other than classical policy documents.

4.3   BRANDING AS MOTIVATING, ACTIVATING, AND BINDING ACTORS

The governance literature stresses that the involvement of stakeholders occurs through negotiation in more horizontal relations between governmental organizations and a wide variety of stakeholders (Rhodes 1997; Pierre 2000). This is the reason why most scholars see a significant difference between governance and government, the former relying on negotiation, whereas the latter relies more strongly on command and control or top-down steering (Rhodes 1997; Kickert et al. 1997; Pierre 2000).

Activating: Rational or Not?

Now although this is certainly relevant, it does not tell the whole story of governance. In the governance literature, there is an implicit emphasis on the rational strategic dimension of the process, including when it comes to the activation and binding of actors. The governance literature is commonly rooted in the idea that actors are activated because they have a strategic interest in the decision-making process, because they have to protect their interests, or because they have to achieve goals they cannot achieve without other actors (see for instance Scharpf 1978, 1997; Benson 1982; Milward and Provan 2000). Although rational and strategic motivations have been shown to be very important in policymaking, the focus on rational aspects has often been at expense of "softer" actor motivations, such as enthusiasm about ideas, the longing to be part of interesting innovative processes, or maybe even the habit of following well-known and long-standing practices.

Another matter relevant to the activation and binding of actors is that actors need to choose selectively what issues they address and what issues they ignore, because actors tend to be very busy, and they operate in crowded interaction areas with multiple policy games and policy arenas (see also March and Olsen 1976). Most actors therefore have too many initiatives and too little time, and consequently they have to choose between initiatives. If we accept that people are not purely rational beings, their choices will probably not be entirely based on a rational weighing of interests, but also on choosing initiatives that catch their attention because they look interesting, attract media attention, or make actors enthusiastic. Thus, besides rational arguments, one can expect emotional attachment to function as an important factor in activating and binding actors.

Governance is, therefore, also about motivating actors with interesting policy content and *seducing* various stakeholders to become active (Koppenjan and Klijn 2004). There is after all nothing to negotiate if crucial actors are not activated and ignore the process. This is where branding can play an interesting role because this is precisely what brands try to do: motivate people to choose this brand over others and bind people to the brand by connecting it and its associations to the desires and feelings of consumers. Brands single out a specific product or, in the case of governance, a specific policy, policy problem, or solution over others and position it as interesting, worthwhile, and important to invest time and energy in.

Activating and Binding on Two Levels: The Possible Role of Branding

Thus we argue that brands can influence two aspects that are crucial to modern governance process: they can activate actors, and they can bind actors in a governance network. Brands can activate actors by triggering emotions (for example making them enthusiastic or angry) and motivating them to act and support the branded policy or project. Actors may be motivated to act by the ideas and values that underlie a brand, or the aspiration that is inherent in the brand. Binding refers to the process whereby actors become attached to the brand over a prolonged period of time. They build a relationship with the brand and feel a certain commitment to it and to the ideas that it conveys. We distinguish between one-off activation and a more prolonged binding of actors. In politics, activation may be about voting; in governance, it may be about giving an opinion or participating in a decision, whereas binding is about becoming engaged in active and prolonged support of a policy or a politician, or about continued efforts to get a particular decision implemented. Both activating and binding can take place on an individual actor level or on a network level. Table 4.2 summarizes the various possibilities. At the network level, binding means that actors not only are loyal but also want to contribute in the sense that they interact with other actors, contribute resources, engage in negotiations, develop solutions, and so forth.

The table differentiates between single actors and networks. When a brand activates or binds (autonomous) singular actors, there is only a relationship between the actor and the brand, and not a relationship among the

Table 4.2   Functions of Brands in Governance Networks

	Actor Level	Network Level
Activating	Actor activation	Network activation
	Single actors are activated because the brand triggers certain emotions and because actors are attracted by the ideas and values of the brand.	Brands can activate multiple actors in a network at the same time, or even activate a network as a whole. Such activation reproduces the network and adds to its viability.
Binding	Actor loyalty	Network loyalty
	Single actors feel attached to the brand and the values behind it. They may build a relationship with the brand and support it over a prolonged period of time.	A network of people feel bound by their shared interest in a particular brand. They feel a relationship because they support the same brand. Thus, a network of actors is loyal to the brand, and this also creates loyalty among the actors themselves since they develop a feeling of connectedness and having a mutual relationship centered around the brand (and contributing to it and the network).

actors around the brand. This is what happens when many actors who do not know each other vote for a particular political party during elections, or when people as individuals support a particular policy. The actor supports the brand but does not actively participate in an actor network around the brand. In the case of network activation or network loyalty, a network of actors around the brand becomes active. But how does this activating and binding work exactly? This is the subject of the next section.

How Brands Can Activate Actors

Brands have the ability to communicate to the various stakeholders, not by rational arguments where policy goals are connected to policy instruments, but by providing images and symbols that construct and communicate brand values, brand identities, and the aspirations that brands represent (Arvidsson 2006; Batey 2008). Thus brands create images of the "good things" that can be achieved, for example better connections (railway projects), improved neighborhoods (urban revitalization projects), or better services (integral services for healthcare). The promise that is inherent in brands shows what can be realized, and this motivates actors. Another aspect of brands that activates is the aspect of emotions. We have dealt with the working of emotions in Chapter 2, and it suffices here to say that emotions such as fear or hope activate cognitive or even bodily processes. For example, humans have a strong biologically ingrained urge to flee when they experience fear (see e.g. Turner 2007).

In short, actors can be triggered by the emotions that a brand evokes and become attracted to the core ideas, values, and associations that come with the brand. For example, the Obama brand, which represented his identity, core ideas, and the promise of change, activated many Americans in the sense that they went out and voted for him. The "New Labour" brand, and the accompanying brands such as the "Third Way," contained aspirations and promises of improving Britain that activated many individuals to support those brands.

Brands can also activate entire networks of actors that feel a common motivation to support the brand and strengthen it. This was visible within the network of the Labour Party when New Labour emerged. This pattern could also be seen in the many local networks of supporters of the Obama brand. Of course, one could question whether the network is activated by the content of the policies or by the brand. We do not mean to argue that the policies themselves do not activate people, but we do argue that the brand has an additional activating function here, for example because the brand can communicate the core values and aspirations of the policies well (if it is a strong brand of course).

In order to fulfill such a function, brands are constructed and marketed in different ways than classical policy documents. Danesi (2006) says that a brand needs: (1) an appropriate name for the product, or in our case for example a policy idea; (2) a suitable logo; (3) slogans that reinforce the brand's image; (4) a design for the product or policy; (5) an advertising text that puts the brand's signification system on display in various ways. The activation of actors occurs through a combination of these elements. The name should evoke a certain enthusiasm and create positive associations. The logo supports the brand and creates associations because it is a more visible component of the brand. Thus the logo should support and strengthen the policy idea.

In many cases, brands evoke various associations, and these associations are not necessarily the same for all stakeholders (Arvidsson 2006). Most brands are designed in such a way that particular associations are facilitated more than others, but the brand's message is usually not detailed or "closed" in the sense that it is completely predetermined. In that respect, brands are different from at least the classical image of policy documents in which clarity and unity of meaning are considered important. Actually, brands try to communicate images for each of their "audiences," or as we would frame it in governance terms: each of the stakeholders. This means that brands have to be able to create different associations and that various stakeholders are able to develop their own mix of associations (see also Kavaratzis and Ashworth 2005).

It is crucial that people create their own meaning for brands and have different associations, as the brand literature emphasizes (e.g. Batey 2008). By extrapolation therefore, branding in governance processes is an attempt to motivate various actors by using images and logos that evoke enough valuable associations to connect to various actors from different backgrounds. This means that brands are images of future states that are ambiguous enough to absorb different opinions among different actors. Or as Arvidsson (2006, 8) states about brands in the private sector: "Brands rather embrace the general principle of what Nicolas Rose (1999) has called 'advanced liberal governance'—they work *with* the freedom of consumers, they say not 'You Must!' but 'You May!'"

Consequently, brands are capable of something that policy documents hardly do: appeal to actors, motivate and activate them in governance processes by enabling them to develop their own associations with the brand, and motivate them to make these associations happen (by buying the branded product or supporting the branded policy). Brands motivate people through what they promise and what can be achieved by the brand (Arvidsson 2006). In that sense, brands communicate in both a more visual and a more open way since the brand is not "finished" but can be developed further, as shown in Chapter 1 with the idea of the Third Way. That makes them especially appropriate for activating actors in governance processes since these are fundamentally open in the sense that none of the actors can predefine or impose a future state. Governance processes are about exploring and negotiating what policy will be formed and realized. Brands as visual images of what could possibly be achieved can motivate actors and draw them into the governance process as we will show in section 4.4 where we analyze public–private partnerships as brands.

How Brands Can Bind Actors

Branding can be considered a continuous process "focused on the creation of value through relationships with all stakeholder groups not just consumers" (Hankinson 2004, 111). It is therefore crucial not only to create the brand but also to establish a relation with stakeholders and create what is called brand loyalty. The fact that consumers stay with the brand (and the product) for a protracted period is one of the important reasons for creating brands in the first place. And this is not only the case in the commercial sector. Needham (2006) argues that political parties have to work harder nowadays to get support from voters and secure a long-term relationship. She argues that brands can help. Brands can be vehicles for relationships with target groups or stakeholders (e.g. Fournier 1998; Hankinson 2004; Needham 2006). In other words, brands can be used to build and maintain relationships with consumers, voters, or citizens. The idea is that brands not only provide an instrument to reduce complexity but also are the basis for ongoing marketing activities of parties and political leaders. Brands can enhance loyalty in several ways if the focus shifts from the product to the relationship with the consumer.

The brand can be developed in such a way that people may develop a relationship with the "brand personality." What is at play here is that public brands are used to highlight branded objects such as public organizations or policy programs, thus accentuating their uniqueness. Thanks to this accentuated identity, people can relate to the branded object in certain ways. In the relationship between product and consumer, "the growing recognition of, and respect for each other's personality would lead to a strong bonding and attitude reinforcement, along with repeat-usage" (De Chernatony and Dall'Olmo Riley 1998, 423). Brands as relationships can be found for example in cases where products are branded as exclusive products. Exclusive brands offer their high status and authority to the owners of branded products, as in a relationship. The brand does something to the psychological and social life of the consumer. As Fournier (1998) has shown, people build relationships with brands that are like relationships with friends and colleagues, whereby brands fulfill similar purposes. People may develop relationships with brands that are comparable to casual friendships, flings, or even secret affairs (Fournier 1998). For example, people may secretly drink liquor of a particular cheap brand, hiding this from others to whom they pretend that they drink expensive brands.

The development of a relationship is facilitated when brands begin to function as sources upon which individuals draw to construct their identity (Elliott and Davies 2006). In such cases, "brands are appropriated by consumers as a means of defining who they are, wish to be and/or wish to be seen as" (Balmer 2006, 36). For example, people may draw on their Apple laptop to further an artistic identity. The brand has a particular identity on which people draw, and to which they feel related. People come to identify themselves (partly) with a brand, for example when they start to see themselves as "a protagonist of the Øresund Bridge," or "a supporter of Obama." Identification with a brand and having a relationship with a brand may lead to prolonged support of the brand and the binding of individuals to the brand.

Brands as relationships highlight the two-way nature of the communication and influence between the brand and the audience. The brand communicates specific messages to the consumer, but there is also communication from the consumer back to the brand or the brand owner. The consumer may influence the brand by explicitly communicating about his or her perception of the brand, or contributing to the further development of the brand. The consumer may also implicitly or unconsciously influence the brand. When consumers with a specific identity use a certain brand, this changes the image of the brand. Thus, consumers become co-producers of the brand (see Arvidsson 2006; Hankinson 2004).

If this perspective is applied in a governance context, it becomes clear that citizens can become involved in the construction of a brand. For example, Barack Obama's campaign motivated large groups of (young) voters to organize their own political activities at the local level. Through these activities, the supporters built a relationship with the Obama brand, and moreover they contributed to the Obama brand, which symbolized Obama as a man of the people. The process of building a brand can co-evolve with the process of binding voters or stakeholders. As elaborated in Chapter 6, this perspective is interesting for both service delivery and governance processes that require the active participation of stakeholders.

So far, we have seen how individuals can build binding relationships with brands, but this is not the whole story. What is equally relevant in governance processes is that brands can bind multiple actors in networks. From marketing in the private sector it is known that brands can enhance the formation of brand communities. This has been underpinned through empirical research in, for example, Saab and Jeep communities (McAlexander et al. 2002; Muniz and O'Guinn 2001). These are communities with members having a "shared consciousness, rituals and traditions, and a sense of moral responsibility" (Muniz and O'Guinn 2001, 412). Members of a brand community define their own identity partly in terms of the brand community to which they belong. Although the degree to which brand communities exist in the public sector has not been established scientifically (more research is needed here), the same kind of mechanisms seem to be at work in the public sector where networks of actors develop around a particular brand such as "cradle to cradle" or "Obama." In some cases, actors develop a feeling that they are sharing something because they feel the same connection to a (public) brand, for example a community such as Brooklyn, or a city such as Berlin, or a particular project that actors are enthusiastic about. The mechanism here is that the shared feeling of being connected to the brand strengthens relationships in the network. From this perspective, brands are situated in the context of relationships between actors in networks, and this draws the brand concept right into the heart of governance in which relationships between actors are so important.

As stated, the common interest in a brand, and the concomitant feeling of loyalty to a brand, may cause mutual identification and the strengthening of relationships in the network. When relationships among people around the brand evolve and become stronger, this further enhances the binding of people to the brand. It becomes hard for people not to be loyal if they feel that this may harm their relationships with the people to whom they feel related. Of course it is not only the brand that binds people, but also the content of a particular project or the political interests that people have in a particular project. However we wish to emphasize that the brand can have a binding function apart from other binding factors.

4. 4   AN EXAMPLE OF BRANDS AS A MOTIVATING CONCEPT: PUBLIC–PRIVATE PARTNERSHIPS

It is time to take the branding perspective to real life policy, and for that we use the issue of public–private partnership (PPP) that has become so prominent in many western countries. There is no doubt that public–private partnerships have been a major issue for quite a long time, now not only in government rhetoric, but also in government practice. In many countries, governments have turned to the idea of public–private partnerships, or partnerships in general, as a vehicle to realize better policy outcomes, or to enhance investments in fields such as infrastructure, health, or social policy (Hodge and Greve 2005). As we will argue in this section, PPP has been used as a brand. The name public–private partnership, and the abbreviation PPP, have deliberately been given a certain meaning that distinguishes PPPs from other institutional arrangements, and the brand has been used to communicate positive things such as cooperation, efficiency, and better governance in general.

A Contested Concept

However, at the same time, the concept and the idea of PPP are contested (see Hodge and Greve 2005; Weihe 2008). Even if we roughly define PPP as a "more or less sustainable cooperation between public and private actors in which joint products and/or services are developed and in which risks, costs, and profits are shared" (Klijn and Teisman 2003, 137), we can still find many different forms under this heading.

The UK version of PPP emanating from the Private Finance Initiative (PFI), for instance, has been dominating the PPP discussion both in practical terms and in scientific terms (see also Weihe 2008). In this version, innovative contracting is the most important element, and partnership is translated into a long-term contractual relationship between a public and a private partner. The literature mentions some reasons why PPP creates added value: because the private partner is able to bid on a more general set of requirements, there is room for innovation and creativity. Also, the private partner can profit from the long-term contract and economize on construction and maintenance (Steijn et al. 2011).

The idea has spread to other countries. The core ideas in the Dutch PPP documentation, for instance, have been taken directly from the British PFI documents (Klijn 2009; see Kenniscentrum PPS 1998, 1999, 2001, 2002); and the OECD documents about PPP (see e.g. OECD 2008) also show direct influence of the UK PFI model. In other countries, however, we can witness a variety of other forms such as Consortia (e.g. urban regeneration companies), intensive general cooperation between public and private actors (for example in policy programs), and network-like partnerships. There are PPPs in which relationships between the partners are more like principal–agent relationships, whereas the relationships are more equal in other PPPs (see S. P. Osborne 2000; Hodge and Greve 2005; Weihe 2008).

PPP as a Brand and Its Associations

Now, if we judge the PPP concept by the classical requirements of policy-making mentioned in section 4.2—logical, clear policy goals underpinned by policy instrument theories and policy field theories—we are likely to be disappointed by the ambiguity of the PPP concept. Under the heading of PPP many different forms of PPPs can be found, and the concept therefore has different meanings in different concrete contexts. However, as a brand, the PPP symbol has fulfilled important functions for those who have used it. Governments have used the PPP concept to "sell" a specific policy and practice, and to communicate with other stakeholders. The different forms of PPPs can be seen as separate manifestations of the brand.

It is not the product (the organizational arrangement) that is most important from a branding point of view, but the identity and aspirations that are communicated with it. So, in the UK, the word partnership was closely linked with Blair's New Labour story. Partnership is about doing things differently, tackling problems together with society and private actors, instead of doing it alone or privatizing it to the market. It holds a promise of both joined-up government (Pollitt 2003) and efficiency. It thus points the way forward and motivates local governments, citizens, non-profit organizations, or private organizations. And it helped Blair to distinguish his policies from other policies, especially those of the Conservatives. Distinguishing is exactly what brands are meant to do. All in all, the PPP brand evokes images and emotions that communicate core values and aspirations. This is the function of the PPP concept, rather than communicating an exact setup or aim for the policy, let alone an exhaustive rational explanation of its working.

We can see this when we look at the real life use of the PPP concept. When establishing an urban renewal corporation (URC), a PPP construction for improving urban areas, the Sandwell Borough in Birmingham clearly uses this image to motivate other actors: "The Sandwell URC will be a highly focused, tasks driven, independent vehicle for driving the large scale, physical economic transformation of the central core of the Arc of opportunity . . . The company will be run in a business like way and will be unfettered by its affiliation to two public sector agencies . . . Fundamental to achieve the Company's aim will be to engage and work in a coordinated manner with other agencies and partnerships with an interest in the physical development of this area."[1]

What we see here is that actors on the local level, especially governmental actors, use the broad PPP brand to distinguish the approach from other approaches, give it additional meaning, and thereby attract extra support. In this way, they profit from the associations that the general PPP brand evokes.

Box 4.2 contains quotes from policy documents, audit reports, and consultant reports that exemplify the associations invoked by the PPP brand.

Box 4.2   Quotes on PPP

The aim for added value is in accordance with the development to a more business-like government. Measures like the introduction of market mechanisms, stimulating efficient forms of buying, and the implementation of privatization and agentification are examples of this. With public–private partnerships, ways are being explored to work more efficiently. Besides the realization of added value by a better cooperation between public and private parties in various phases of a project, the government wants to achieve added value by a more efficient form of financing. . . . the financial instruments are shaped in such a way that central government is reimbursed for some of the financial investments, while at the same time private firms achieve higher financial results. (Kenniscentrum PPS 1999, 11)This arrangement means that the same partners are potentially involved in a long term relationship over the whole contract life . . . By integration of the design and construction elements bidders are encouraged to take a longer term view of the design of the asset . . . that will reduce maintenance costs throughout the contract period. (NAO 2003, 4)The PFI has many advantages. It enables public sector organisations to spread the costs of infrastructure investment over the lifetime of the asset, avoiding some of the uncertainties present in conventional procurement. In addition, because the payments mechanism is aligned with the project objectives, PFI offers improved likelihood of projects being on time, to budget, and meeting the original specifications. It also encourages a focus on value for money over the lifetime of the asset. (Deloitte 2006, 3)PPPs have proved their worth by bringing about improvements in public service quality through shorter delivery times, better value for money and increased innovation through the use of competition across a range of sectors. (CBI 2007, 4)Governments introduce PPPs for several reasons: to improve the value for money in public service delivery, or because PPP has the potential of bringing private finance to public service delivery. Leaving the design to the private partner creates room for the private partner to be innovative in its design and thereby improve the level of efficiency of the service (OECD 2008).

How is the PPP brand constructed, and what associations does it generate if we look at the quotes in Box 4.2? The brand provides additional value because it enhances the approach with promises of efficiency and extra knowledge. The business-like description in the above quote of the Sandwell borough council is a clear example of that; as is the promise of improved cooperation between the public and the private sphere. The concept of PPP not only adds value but also gives meaning and creates associations. The associations include handling problems in a different way where the knowledge of public partners and private partners are combined (see Kenniscentrum 2001, 2002; NAO 2002). Actually, the only element in which PPP is somewhat lacking is the visual image, since the brand is more connected with the name than with a clear slogan or visual.

Not surprisingly, PPP became an important element of New Labour politics because the above-mentioned associations fit very well with the ideas of New Labour and the Third Way; the problem is not government as such (as Thatcher said), but the way government works together with society and the private sector. The irony was of course that PPP had already been initiated by the Conservatives but was relaunched and rebranded by Labour (see Klijn et al. 2007).

PPP Brand as Activating, Motivating, and Binding, but Also Ambiguous

From a brand point of view, therefore, it is the meaning and identity that matters rather than the product itself, although of course there has to be a link between the two (Hankinson 2004). Thus partnership, and public–private partnership, are used in quite different ways by different governments, in different countries, and so forth, in an attempt to create the right image (and connected emotion) that will do the trick of communicating a policy aim, reach and activate interested investors, and reassure the public that this is good, solid policymaking and implementation. The PPP brand can activate actors in the sense that it provides an interesting new idea to which actors may feel attached and consequently become active. This is especially the case for private actors that will become more motivated and activated to engage in cooperation with (local) governments; and once they are involved in a partnership they are also bound to the network of the partnership by contracts, loyalty to the idea, and mutual dependencies. PPP therefore helps to engage private actors in a specific governance network around service delivery, infrastructure, or other public tasks.

Note that different stakeholders have different associations with the terms partnerships or public–private partnerships. In the classical view of public administration this is a problem, but from a brand point of view it is not really a problem. Ambiguity is even necessary to motivate as many different actors as possible. The more the partnership construction is specified beforehand, the more likely it is that disagreement will arise about it. Involved actors will have different views on problems, profit, division of risks, and so forth that will cause conflict and possible deadlocks. The PPP brand must be able to absorb all these complexities, and thus a certain amount of ambiguity is useful. Ambiguity creates the possibility for different actors to embrace the idea despite the fact that they do not agree on several aspects; and that is precisely one of the strong points and advantages of a brand in governance processes: because of its ambiguity and its emotional value, it can bind different actors and connect them.

4.5 CONCLUSIONS

This chapter has shown how brands can motivate, activate, and bind actors in governance processes. This is a crucial function in governance processes where parties are dependent on each other and need to appeal to others. Governance processes are simply impossible to bring to satisfactory outcomes without the involvement of (crucial) stakeholders.

However, these stakeholders have to be activated and motivated to at least support initiatives. Another step is to bind them to the governance processes in the sense that they actively engage in interaction and show loyalty. Binding actors is especially important since governance is often about processes of developing joint solutions for seemingly intractable problems instead of setting solutions at the start of the process.

Brands can motivate and activate stakeholders by providing interesting ideas and appealing associations about future states and attractive prospects. In that sense, they can be helpful to preclude opposition and the use of veto power by stakeholders. When actors develop a relationship with a brand (for example a political party with an identity to which people feel attracted), the brand not only activates but also binds actors.

Whereas the governance literature tends to emphasize that actors are activated and bound because they have a strategic interest in a decision-making process, brands activate and bind actors more through other motivations such as enthusiasm about ideas, or the wish to be part of interesting innovative processes. The idea behind branding is that the brand holds promises that are appealing and motivate actors.

5 Brands and the Media
Communicating with the Outside World

5.1 BRANDS AND THE ROLE OF MEDIA
IN GOVERNANCE PROCESSES

On 6 October 2008 the bank accounts of ICESAVE in Iceland are suddenly no longer accessible to customers in the UK and the Netherlands. ICESAVE was a savings brand of the Icelandic bank, Landsbanki, which was rolled out in several European countries in a relatively short time. Most of its customers were attracted from the UK and the Netherlands, although the bank was also active in other countries. ICESAVE was a relative newcomer on the savings market and attracted people with relatively high interest rates (5.5 percent).

In the days before the accounts become inaccessible, the media become increasingly alarmed about the Icelandic economy and the problems with Icelandic banks. On 5 October, British newspapers mention doubts about the stability of the banks, saying that "it remains to be seen whether they will be resilient enough" (*Sunday Times* 2008). Other newspapers present the situation as almost disastrous. *The Observer* writes that "the party's over for Iceland" (*The Observer* 2008). They write about a free fall of the Icelandic currency, suggesting a process that is out of control. They compare Iceland to countries such as Zimbabwe and Turkmenistan, and mention serious problems with three major Icelandic banks (*The Observer* 2008). Not surprisingly, many customers get worried. ICESAVE tries to maintain the impression that it is able to deal with the problems, and it tries to rescue its image because loss of that might cause a bank run. For example on 7 October, when the bank accounts are no longer accessible, a spokeswoman for the bank says that the website of the online bank is not operating due to technical difficulties (BBC 2008). However, the alarming messages emanating from the media make such statements unbelievable to most customers. The former owner of the bank, Gudmundsson, states that the bank's assets are sufficient to repay all depositors at ICESAVE (Iceland Review Online 2008). Despite such messages, the bank does not succeed in maintaining the image of being able to solve the problems. Depositors have become extremely worried, and rightly so as it turns out after a few chaotic days during which developments evolve like a rollercoaster out of control.

Inevitably, it becomes clear that Landsbanki is in severe financial difficulties, and it can no longer guarantee its depositors' savings. To solve the problem and retain the reserves that are still with the bank, the Icelandic government unilaterally nationalizes the bank and divides the reserves in two.

The Landsbanki problems attract a lot of media attention, and dramatic stories are told of individual savers who seem to have lost all their money; and in both countries a huge commotion emerges because it is not only individual savers that have deposited money with Landsbanki (in the UK, 300,000 customers with a total amount of about 4 billion pounds; in the Netherlands, 125,000 customers with a total amount of 1.7 billion Euros); a number of local governments both in the UK and in the Netherlands have also placed large sums of money with ICESAVE.

The ICESAVE problems, partly because of the extensive media attention, also provoke strong reactions in the Dutch and British parliaments and national governments. The immense media attention makes it very important to the political parties and governments in both the UK and the Netherlands to show that they are taking the issue seriously and that they are doing everything they can to protect the interests of their constituencies. MPs get most of their information and reasons to ask questions from the media. Of all the parliamentary questions asked in the Netherlands about ICESAVE, 75 percent originate from media news (Vogelaar 2010). This includes newspaper articles and TV programs that honed in on the ICESAVE case. The national governments also react strongly. Just ten minutes after the nationalization of the banks, the UK government uses its Anti-terrorism, Crime and Security Act of 2001 to freeze all assets belonging to Landsbanki and assets belonging to the Central Bank of Iceland. The UK prime minister, Gordon Brown, voices strong discontent with the measures taken by the Iceland government, and he announces that the UK government will launch legal action against Iceland. Whether it was because of the media pressure or not, the Dutch government and Iceland agree on 10 October to work together to reach a solution. This proves to be slightly more difficult. The constant media pressure in the UK and the Netherlands, but also in Iceland where public opinion shifts more and more towards the feeling that "we as citizens are not responsible for the irresponsible behavior of a firm in Iceland," makes the negotiation process extremely difficult.

After negotiations in June 2009, an agreement is reached in which the UK and the Netherlands provide the money for the customers who lost their savings, and the Icelandic government is to pay that money back. However, media and public commotion about the deal in Iceland lead the president to refuse to sign it, and a referendum is organized to give the people a voice in whether or not to accept it. The vast majority of Icelanders reject the deal and are not prepared to pay the price for a bank's mistakes. These feelings continue to exist even after the parliaments of the three countries come to an agreement in 2010 about repayment (under less severe conditions). The agreement has been rejected twice in a referendum by the Icelandic people (in 2010 and 2011).

Media Affecting Actions in Governance Processes

The ICESAVE case is an example of the importance of the media, whose activities proceed in many ways:

1. *Political pressure and political attention*: The constant media pressure forces the political leaders in the UK and the Netherlands to follow the process closely, and to make firm stands and statements. But the media have other influences on political decision making, in the sense that the media inform politicians and civil servants about what is going on. This phenomenon is not restricted to this case alone. Media news has increasingly become the main information source for political action (see Elchardus 2002; Fischer 2003).

2. *Intervention in the interaction process*: Media attention also directly influences the interaction process. It complicates the delicate negotiations, creates unexpected dynamics in the interactions, and thus increases complexity. The media coverage in Iceland itself for instance puts pressure on Icelandic politicians to show that they are not the dupes of Britain and the Netherlands, and that they listen to the Icelandic people. This leads to complications when the president of Iceland decides not to accept the agreement between Iceland, the UK, and the Netherlands, but to organize a referendum on the agreement among the Icelandic population. So media attention influences actors' actions in the process.

3. *Media as vehicles to protect or damage brand integrity*: In this case, but also in other governance processes that go through a period of crisis, we witness another phenomenon. That is, actors try to damage each other's brands and image of integrity, and try to protect their own brand. Now, banks are in themselves a brand that must signify integrity and especially trust. If the brand of a bank no longer stands for reliability, if it is no longer trusted, depositors might start withdrawing their money. If the media start reporting about this process, adding that the bank seems to be in trouble, more people may become anxious, and a bank run may occur. If the brand fails and people demand their money all at once, most banks fail. Media attention is crucial in creating, maintaining, or destroying brands of organizations, leaders, products, or countries. Banks are well aware of this and they try to protect themselves by communicating reassuring messages in the media. Politicians are also very attentive to how they are pictured in the media (Fischer 2003; Bennett 2009). Politicians react directly and strongly to the news in the media in order to establish and sustain their image of strong and decisive leaders. The example in Box 5.1 shows a remarkable example of this in the ICESAVE case.

Box 5.1   Media and Political Intervention in the ICESAVE Case

How important media appearance is for sustaining an actor's brand can be shown by an example, in this case coming from the Dutch side. The minister of finance, Wouter Bos, has communicated from the beginning that the Dutch government will solve the problem for the individual Dutch customers of ICESAVE, but at the same time in Tthe Netherlands, just as in the UK, a number of local governments and provinces also had large sums of money placed with ICESAVE/Landsbanki. These organize themselves and stress that they will pursue a separate claim if central government does not promote their interest. On 31 October 2008, the provincial CEO of the province of North Holland, who acts as spokesperson for the group of governmental actors, is a guest on a political late night discussion program on TV. He tells the interviewer that the group is not very satisfied with the Dutch government and that they are thinking of sending in a separate claim to get their money back. Suddenly, in the middle of the broadcast, Minister Bos calls the program and tells the interviewer that this is not true. The minister explains that individual customers have preference over the local and provincial governments, who should have enough slack to cope with the financial losses. He stresses that he does not want to complicate or hinder the complex negotiations with extra claims from the local governments and makes very clear that he would certainly stop the local governments. The minister humiliates the provincial CEO and crushes his image during the broadcast. He portrays himself as a decisive leader who knows how and when to take action. It is a remarkable action since it has never been done before during a media event. It shows how much politics and the images of leaders are constructed and influenced by media events and activities. In this case, a political dispute was not so much represented by the media; rather, it took place within the media. One could argue that the TV program was not only an intermediary passing on information, but also an arena in which policymaking took place. One could also argue that the media are no longer purely an outside factor that influences governance processes, but have become part of the very fabric of governance processes (cf. Hepp et al. 2010).

Exploring Media Influence in Governance and the Relevance of Brands

Media influence has increased considerably not only on the daily life of citizens but also on political and administrative processes. This chapter explores this increasing influence (section 5.2) and elaborates the relation between media and governance processes (section 5.3). It argues that the rise of brands in the private and public sphere is strongly related to the rise of the media because brands have certain qualities that are important in the media, for example their intensive use of visual images, strong associations, and emotional content that catches attention (section 5.4). We argue that these qualities very much fit the media logic these days of newspapers, (commercial) TV stations, and Internet media.

5.2   THE RISE OF MEDIA INFLUENCE AND SOME OF ITS CONSEQUENCES

Our everyday life has become much more dominated by the media, especially TV and social media, than say 30 or 40 years ago. People spend more time in front of various media, especially the TV (Bennett 2009; Lundby 2009). The media have become the most important source of information for citizens nowadays (Strömbäck and Esser 2009).

At the same time, the quantity of what can be called hard news (news that is not presented as personal news), and news that deals with the wider background of events (not news about today's shootings in Iraq but historical news about the cause of the war) are diminishing. Also, the classical carriers of information such as newspapers are being read less and less, especially by younger generations. Bennett (2009) shows that each generation of young people over the last 40 years has consumed less news than the previous one.

Thus we see three movements at the same time. Firstly, the media, especially TV and the Internet, have become more important in everyday life. One can say that the media, especially TV and recently also the Internet, increasingly determine how we see and construct everyday life. Secondly, information in the media has changed, as the media have come to work according to a specific media logic. Thirdly, the relationship between the media, politics, and society has changed. Below, we first elaborate on media logic, and then on the changing relationship between the media, politics, and society.

Media Logic: Personalized and Dramatized News in a Commercial Environment

Zooming in on media logic we can distinguish three interrelated aspects of media logic: informational logic involving bias in the content of media messages, organizational logic (often related to commercialization), and the usage of fixed formats in the presentation of news.

Patterson's (2000) analysis of 5,000 news stories between 1980 and 1999 shows a significant change in both the subject of news and the way news is presented. Stories without public policy-related content increased from 35 percent to nearly 50 percent of all news. Other soft news about, for example, crime and human interest, rose significantly from 20 to 40 percent, (crime-related stories from 8 to 14 percent, human interest from 10 to 25 percent) (Patterson 2000). Several scholars report a dramatic change in the content of the news. There is more focus on dramatic stories, less on public policy issues, and for instance a strong decline in international news, apart from dramatic events like large wars or terrorist attacks (see Bennett 2009; Strömbäck and Esser 2009).

Authors emphasize the growing commercialization of news (especially in the US and the UK), with mergers and ownership consolidation in the news industry. More than ever, news has become big business. There is a strong need to make profits and capture large portions of the TV audience, since large numbers guarantee good incomes from advertising. This has stimulated the increase in what has been labeled as soft news, that is, emotional and immediate news, which is largely meant to be entertaining. Bennett (2009) shows that the focus on crime, an important form of soft news, has increased significantly. He reports that between 1990 and 1998 the number of crime stories broadcasted on the NBC, CBS, and ABC programs rose from 542 to 1,392. During that time, however, actual levels of most violent crimes dropped (Bennett 2009, 25). The number of murder stories rose by 700 percent between 1993 and 1996, despite a drop of 20 percent in the actual figures. Bennett then goes on to argue that 70 percent of the people in the US get their information about crime from TV, whereas only 20 percent get such information from newspapers. Thus not only is news, especially TV, very important for shaping people's opinions, but the pressure on the media to make a profit and attract large audiences seems to significantly bias what is actually disseminated on the news.

Bennett (2009) recognizes four types of informational biases that are the result of recent developments in the media:

1. *Personalization*: There is strong tendency in the news to emphasize the personal aspect of news and downplay the wider social, economic, or political context in which the reported events take place. As Shanahan et al. (2008, 120) argue, there is a "desire for storytelling, which intrigues the reader with individual characters strategically portrayed as heroes, villains, and victims." The idea is that, when news is framed in more personal ways, it appeals more to readers and viewers. Take for example George W. Bush announcing the end of the Iraq war in 2003, already mentioned in Chapter 3. Most media personalized the event by focusing on Bush as a leader and his personal battle (see Bennett 2009); but in doing that they tended to ignore or downplay other aspects such as the fact that Bush's military past was not that impressive. Also, they tended to blur the far greater complexity of the Iraq war. Thus personalization tends to eclipse the larger complexity issues.

2. *Dramatization and emotionalization*: There is also a tendency to dramatize news and emphasize stories that focus on crisis and conflict

rather than on continuity or harmony. Crises are very suitable for dramatization in the media because they contain sequences of sudden actions in which actors' characters appear more sharply. The recent trend of providing live images of events as they happen has reinforced the trend towards dramatization. Dramatization is visible, for instance, in the tendency to frame the primaries for the US presidential election as horse races with winners and losers, with "dark horses" suddenly putting in a sprint and unexpected winners (see Bennett 2009). This simplifies the facts and creates an urge to overstate facts. For instance, Hillary Clinton was already almost proclaimed the new president of the US before the primaries for the 2008 presidential election even started. Her loss of the first primary was presented as a great blow. Both claims overstated the real situation because few voters determine their preferences before the primaries.

3. *Fragmentation*: The news has a growing tendency to focus on isolate stories and events and separate them from the larger context and from each other, Bennett (2009) claims. This trend is closely tied to the other two trends. Personalizing the news separates it from its broader societal context. Fragmentation results in complex backgrounds of problems being less well covered, thus making the problem often appear more simple (and more simple to solve!) than it really is.

4. *The authority-disorder bias*: By this, Bennett means that news is preoccupied with disorder and whether authorities are capable of maintaining or restoring order. At the same time, a shift has taken place from an attitude where the media were favorable to politicians and authorities towards an attitude where the media are suspicious of authorities. Patterson (2000) shows that the negative news coverage of politicians in the US has strongly increased (by 1990, negative coverage was over 80 percent). Each president since 1976—Carter, Reagan, Bush, and Clinton—received more negative attention than the previous one. Thus, the media tend to emphasize disorder and authorities who are often incapable of restoring order.

Although the first two biases are the most important and also often stressed by other authors (Mazzoleni and Schulz 1999; Strömbäck and Esser 2009), the other biases are also important in tracing the influence of media on governance processes. The four biases influence both the way policy problems are framed and the attention policy problems receive, but they have also a significant influence on the behavior of politicians, as we shall see later.

But media logic has not only a content dimension as indicated above. Two other dimensions are less well covered in the literature. These dimensions have to do with the internal organization of the media, which is strongly connected to the commercializing of the media, and the use of fixed formats. Several authors point out that the *organization of the media* has changed dramatically in the past 20 years. The rise of commercial TV and the emergence of free newspapers created a huge expansion of TV and newspaper activity. At the same time, most of these media have to make a profit so there is strong pressure to cut costs, and use information that is available or easily accessible (see e.g. Davies 2008). Public broadcasting organizations in Europe, where TV stations are often publicly financed, are also under pressure to trim their budgets. So that means for instance fewer reporters on various sites, and more reliance on news from the few large press associations (Davies 2008). Research shows that the significant bias in the news in newspapers and TV stations has to do with the locations where the reporters are, covering more news from those places than from places where they are not present (Bennett 2009). Thus the internal (and external) organization of media such as TV and newspapers has a significant influence of what has been termed media logic. Or as Bennett (2009, 223) states when he discusses the concentration trends in the media: "And so, today, the news must perform like the entertainment divisions, with profit cutting away at staff and other resources. The first effect of merger pressures on news content typically comes from budget cuts, which often result in staff reductions and the cutting down of expensive international news bureaus. . . . The next common pattern following megamerger is generally a rebranding of the news. . . . The role of news in contemporary brand logic is tied to attracting the right demographic audience to generate the greatest profits." Davies (2008) argues that budget cuts force newspapers to produce the same amount of news with fewer journalists. They have come to depend more on "wire copy," which involves copying texts from press associations and official press releases. This development leads to dominance of the news by a few organizations, pressure to cover events less critically, a shift to infotainment formats, strong emphasis on packaging, branding, and segmenting news to target groups (see Bennett 2009, 325; Davies 2008; Soberman 2005).

The third and last dimension of media logic relates to the use of standard *formats* in the media for news. This has to do with the need to fit the news not only into short, attractive packages, but also into repeated broadcasting times and formats. An example of the influences of standard formats is for instance the need to "fill the hole": news stations assign reporters to certain news items, and these are under pressure to constantly update the news at the times that news broadcasts are planned (the 1 o'clock news, the 5 o'clock news, and so on). But of course there are not always new developments to report. This leads to repeating old news, to journalists asking leading questions that enhance the possibility of reporting interesting new quotes, to speculation or the use of fixed formats in which the news is communicated ("Political leader X denied the rumors today that . . ."). Other fixed formats that put pressure on the news are working to deadlines (better half the story on time than the whole story too late) and the tendency to use the same sources for the news (in the case of the US: the

White House, the State Department, and the Pentagon; see Bennett 2009), resulting also in various news organizations producing the same news and the same quotes.

TV programs also have fixed formats, for example shows in which every guest, including politicians, plays a certain game and also gets 30 seconds to say something about politics.

In fact, these three dimensions of media logic develop mainly in ways that are not only strongly interrelated but also tend towards the same direction. That direction as a whole is a stronger orientation to dramatization and personalization, a need to collect information and communicate it under pressure of time and scarcity, and the need for constant updates that are framed and molded in ways that fit segmented groups in the audience.

Mediatization of Politics and Society?

Interconnected to the debate on media logic and the effect this has on the production of information within the media, there is a heated debate in the literature about media influence on society in general and on politics in particular (see e.g. Hepp et al. 2010; Mazzoleni and Schulz 1999). This is generally termed as the mediatization of politics (or even of society). Mediatization is more than just the fact that the media are the intermediaries of information between for instance politicians and citizens. Mediatization focuses firstly on the way that the media have a deeply structuring influence on politics. Medium theories in particular "describe socio-cultural change as deeply structured by the advent of a new leading medium" (Hepp et al. 2010, 223). It is an important question, for example, whether Twitter structurally influences ways of policymaking by allowing politicians to immediately see how citizens are reacting to certain policy ideas. Secondly, mediatization is about informational effects of the media: how do the media themselves shape and determine the information they disseminate and the way it is interpreted? Thus, if the TV channels determine the shape of the political debate, the subjects, and the way they are discussed, it can be concluded that the media have a real and genuine influence on the way information is created and communicated.

Some scholars stress that the media by now has become an institution in itself, or a subsystem that is separate from, but interdependent with, for instance, the political system with its own rules and logic. This has to do with the commercializing of the media and the media logic just discussed. Others view the media as something that has become part and parcel of the political system (cf. Hepp et al. 2010). In either case, a crucial issue is the extent to which media characteristics become entangled with the political and governance systems as the media system grows in importance. Media become the dominant "environment" (Strömbäck and Esser 2009) or an essential factor for political and administrative actions. When the media become more dominant as the only source of information, the media logic described in the previous section begins to influence or even dominate information gathering and even problem construction, thus starting to have an impact on how other subsystems (especially the political system) function. Multiple scholars have argued that mediatization is an ongoing process now, and that the influence of media logic on other subsystems is high (Mazzoleni and Schulz 1999; Fischer 2003; Bennett 2009). Strömbäck and Esser (2009, 215) go deeper into this issue, explaining that mediatization is high when:

- media constitute the most important and dominant source of information for other activities (e.g. political decisions and governance processes);
- media are strongly independent of other systems (such as the political system) and thus are not influenced by these systems or at least not much;
- media content is governed more by media logic than by any other factor;
- political actors (or other actors in society we would argue) are more dominated by media logic than by their own logic (for example political logic) or, as we would add, their own logic is heavily infused by elements of media logic.

Although the extent of media influence is disputed, there is little doubt that it has grown considerably in the last decades. Political images and political lives, but also complex governance processes, are influenced and shaped by it; or, as Bennett (2009) says, it is important for a politician nowadays to "feed" the media and interact with them because politicians' images have become largely dependent on media appearance. Politicians who reject this advice have severe problems in sustaining their position. Other research affirms this, indicating that the practices of politicians are largely influenced by the media, but at the same time politicians try to retain control over the media by interacting closely with them (Driessens et al. 2010). Hajer (2009) argues that politicians' authority largely depends on how they perform in the media. No wonder that politicians and administrators try to manage and stage the media attention around their policy ideas, their actions, and their brands. The above-mentioned example of President Bush announcing the end of the Iraq war dramatically staged on the aircraft carrier is such an example. The case of ICESAVE at the start of this chapter where the Dutch minister of finance interrupted a live television broadcast is another example. Thus, the growing importance of the media in shaping citizens' perceptions also results in politicians actively trying to shape those images in the media or even creating events with the sole purpose of capturing media attention.

In other words, the growing importance of the media has the effect of politicians attempting to stage events and attract media attention (Mazzoleni and Schulz 1999; Bennett 2009). Bennett describes numerous occasions where politicians create media events and try to "stage" their image and actions through the media. On the one hand, one could consider this as a counter argument against the mediatization of politics, because politicians use media to frame (political) events, meanings, and support; but, on the other hand, this can be seen as an ultimate form of mediatization because politicians are adapting their practices and stories to fit the media logic (e.g. Driessens et al. 2010).

5.3 MEDIA AND GOVERNANCE: OLD THEMES, NEW ISSUES

This growing influence of the media on our everyday life cannot remain without consequences for political life and administrative processes. Since we are looking at the influence of the media on governance, we have to distinguish various ways in which the media can influence governance processes. Much has been written so far about the relation between the media and politics, but there is not so much literature about the relation between the media and governance processes.

Front Stage and Backstage of Governance Processes

Political actors and their decisions are certainly part of the whole governance process, but they do not cover the entire process. It is characteristic of governance that it involves complex interaction and decision-making processes within networks of a wide variety of actors (see Chapter 1). Political actors are important in such processes, but they are not the only actors. One could say that the political arena that is made visible through media attention represents the "front stage" of governance processes. It is the stage where contestation over values is visible to the public. Less visible to the public are the complex interactions between various actors in governance networks; this represents the "backstage" of governance processes, which generally does not come under media scrutiny. However, the media can influence what actors do front stage, and this then influences the backstage activities.

In the next sections, we explore the influence of the media on governance by highlighting three perspectives: (1) the drama democracy perspective, to highlight the influence of the media on the nature of democracy; (2) the perspective of classical agenda-setting theories, to explain the influence of the media on the formation of issues and policy problems; (3) the governance networks perspective, to explore the direct influence of the media on strategic interactions in governance processes.

Drama Democracy and Politics: Mediatized Politics and Governance

The democratic political process seems to have become a drama democracy, to use a term coined by the Belgian social scientist Elchardus (2002). He has shown that news and media processes have become more important in the democratic political process. In addition, the news has become more personalized and individuals have taken on more importance. On the other hand, and linked to this, politics has become more and more theatrical and the dramaturgical dimension has become crucial (Hajer 2009). Politics has become a question of "who can make his/her claim authoritative in the scenes and at the stages that matter in the age of mediatization" (Hajer 2009, 4). In the drama democracy, with its focus on individuals and powerful imagery, politicians perform acts in front of cameras. It is crucial for politicians to direct their performances and avoid being "demonized" in the media. A slip of the tongue, a strong one-liner, or a mistake can be instantly placed on media such as YouTube, and become widely known if it becomes a hit on YouTube. Thus politicians' images have become crucial for their performance, their effectiveness, and their political survival as various authors have observed (Edelman 1988; Elchardus 2002; Fischer 2003).

Leaders try to communicate an image of a strong leader that suits a personalized, media-political world. However, the risks facing strong leaders are high, because it is hard to fulfill the high hopes placed upon strong leaders. Citizens tire easily of their stars in a drama democracy. In a drama democracy, governing means communicating continuously, and policy announcements become more important than policy implementation. After all, policy announcements are news in a drama democracy, whereas the implementation is much less newsworthy, except when things go wrong. Implementation is risky because one can make enemies during the execution and be damaged by problems that occur during implementation. Elchardus defines the rules of a drama democracy as follows: "In a drama democracy it is tempting to score via communication and representation. That is usually easier than clearing files and taking decisions, activities with which one always has the possibility of making enemies. A communication strategy takes the place of ideology, announcing measures takes the place of taking measures, convincing language replaces a supportive concept" (Elchardus 2002, 82; see also Luyendijk 2006 on how news is made).

Elchardus' remarks echo the earlier analyses of Edelman in the 1970s. Edelman (1977, 1988) talked about "words that succeed, policies that fail," by which he wanted to indicate that politics is mainly a verbal game, the actual outcomes of which are not really important. Following Edelman, other authors have also used this image. Fischer's (2003) representation resembles that of Elchardus and Edelman quite closely. He states: "Politicians and the media, as Edelman has shown, have turned contemporary politics into a political spectacle that is experienced more like a stage drama than reality itself. Based on socially constructed stories designed more to capture the interest of the audience than to offer factual portrayal of events, the political spectacle is constructed by a set of political symbols and signifiers that continuously construct and reconstruct self-conceptions, the meaning of past events, expectations for the future, and the significance of prominent social groups. . . . The spectacle of politics is a modern-day fetish, a creation in part of political actors that come to dominate the thoughts and activities of both its audience and the actors themselves" (Fischer 2003, 58).

The rules and practices of the drama democracy seem to clash with the everyday practice of governance networks. In the everyday reality of governance processes, decision making takes place within complex processes in which stakeholders, including groups of citizens, attempt to intervene, or at least to become involved. This is where politics is conducted intensively, but not always recognizably, and where processes require long-term dedication and a lot of network management in order to bring them to a favorable conclusion.

On the other hand, the politics visible to the media and the citizen takes place more and more in an almost surreal media landscape that requires powerful imagery, quick decision making, and clear steering. This sometimes leads to strong intervention in complex processes, which often backfires. Politicians intervene in complex network-like processes through what they consider to be powerful measures, and in doing so are more likely to disrupt the results that have already been achieved (Elchardus 2002; Klijn 2008a). Thus, the rules of the drama democracy, the stress on theater, quick communication, and individuals, seem to clash with those of complex decision-making processes in governance networks. Complex policy processes usually take a long time, many unexpected events can occur, and a lot can go wrong. Due to their complexity, long duration, and slow evolvement they are not easily communicated in terms of fast, simple measures. This is where branding is used; as we elaborate further in section 5.4, branding allows politicians to communicate with the media in a relatively easy way by presenting visual and clear images. Brands are accommodated to some of the main rules of the drama democracy, and they can be used to represent complex problems through more simple and appealing associations.

Media and Agenda Setting: The Classical Perspective on Media

The second way in which media activities influence governance processes is by influencing or even setting the political and administrative agenda. Of course this is not a new insight. The 1970s literature on agenda forming was already addressing how and why certain issues enter the political agenda, paying attention to the use of symbols and the mass media in the creation of coalitions and political support. Cobb and Elder (1983) discuss several strategies to generate more attention for a policy issue, and, in many of them, the application of symbols in the mass media is important. The key to success for these strategies is to put the appeal in a symbolic context that will have a maximum impact on followers, potential supporters, the opposition, or the decision makers. Each strategy is dependent to some extent on the amount of attention provided by the mass media. Symbols and the mass media are two key mechanisms by which groups can channel their demands to a wider constituency and enhance their chances of success (Cobb and Elder 1983, 150).

Other agenda theories also stress the importance of the media as a factor that influences the emergence of issues on the agenda and the way they are connected to solutions. Kingdon (1984) presents a model in which he distinguishes three different streams in decision making: the problem stream, the solution stream, and the political stream. The media are an important component of the last stream. Decisions are taken when the three separate streams of events are connected to each other. Thus, when policy problems, policy solutions, and political events come together in what Kingdon calls a policy window, important decisions are being made. Policy entrepreneurs can facilitate and stimulate that kind of connection, and the media can be a platform on which certain connections are presented and highlighted. Part of the entrepreneurial work is to catch media attention and create a platform in the media and political life for certain issues and policy problems. This is also stressed by Baumgartner and Jones (2009), who emphasize the importance of media attention in bringing certain policy issues to the fore. They also suggest that media attention can be dynamic and important in breaking long-existing, seemingly stable, equilibriums of policymaking and implementation around issues. It is our contention that creating brands may be one of the activities employed to attract attention and keep it when the political mood starts to shift. We elaborate on this issue in section 5.4.

Media and Governance Processes: Influencing the Interaction Process

The two previously discussed media influences—drama democracy and agenda setting—are both, in a sense, indirect influences on governance processes. They influence the interaction process through political intervention or by influencing the political agenda and the way problems are constructed. But media interventions also influence governance processes directly. This happens when governance processes themselves are part of the news and are represented in, commented on, or criticized in the media. In that situation, media intervention affects the perceptions and strategies of the actors involved in governance processes. Media intervention can thus change perceptions of stakeholders who are directly involved in a governance process, for instance on the nature of the problem, and this will result in changed strategies. Given the importance of the media in modern society (regarding the provision of information about ongoing developments and also their great influence on the image and reputation of actors), stakeholders will be inclined to act fairly quickly. Consequently, media attention and intervention may often lead to strategic actions on the part of the involved actors.

This has several indirect results in governance processes. The first is that it will probably increase the complexity and dynamics of the governance processes themselves. Since actors will increase their strategic activity, and this strategic interaction will become more unpredictable, processes will become more uncertain and complex. This also will increase the need to manage interactions. Thus, the overall effect of media intervention is a higher level of activity in governance networks. Under the media spotlight, governance networks become more complex and dynamic.

But given the discussion on the development of the media in section 5.2, with a strong emphasis on negative news and scrutinizing whether the authorities are able to maintain and restore order, one may expect negative interventions to predominate over positive interventions. In a governance context, which commonly involves value conflicts, heightened media attention may put pressure on the process. It may stir up particular conflicts and be disruptive to processes in which parties are slowly coming to an agreement. Especially if there are a substantial number of actors who are not satisfied with the results achieved so far, or with the direction in which the decisions are heading, one might expect them to use media attention to further their interests. Dissatisfied actors might use negative media attention to win support for their values to have a more dominant position in the decision-making process and its outcomes. This may cause new dynamics and strategic uncertainty in the governance process, which in turn increases complexity.

Yet another reason why media attention enhances the complexity of governance processes is the tendency among journalists to seek out new dramatic stories, publish them, and repeat them. Baumgartner and Jones (2009, 106), in their research on agenda setting and the role of media in that, write: "These features of journalistic homogeneity imply positive feedback: with each success in attracting the attention of new media outlets, still more are likely to become interested." Media attention is thus a process that increases and strengthens itself, which then increases the chance that stakeholders and politicians will react to it. This may in turn affect another aspect of the governance network: the patterns of interactions and the level of trust. With regard to trust in particular, it can have an important influence. Trust requires interaction between actors and a build-up of confidence that actors will abide by the agreements, respect one another's values and interests, and give one another the benefit of the doubt (see Edelenbos and Klijn 2007; Eshuis 2006; Klijn, Edelenbos et al. 2010). Negative media attention puts more pressure on the separate actors to harden their points of view, because they have to explain their point of view to the public and defend their position (especially if the media represent the negotiation game in terms of winners and losers). Media attention may then also put pressure on past agreements; and the prospect of possibly breaking earlier agreements (whether written or not) puts pressure on the trust relations between the actors in the governance network.

So there are several mechanisms through which media interventions influence governance processes. One can imagine that media attention has positive effects (enhancing attention for an issue and raising money and support), but there may very well be complicating or negative influences as well. Actually, some scare research carried out on this topic (see Kortha-gen et al. 2011) confirms this. That research, a survey where respondents could indicate the level of media attention and its nature (negative-positive), shows significant negative effects of negative media attention on perceived outcomes of governance processes. The research showed however that we do not see a direct effect of negative media attention on outcomes. Negative media attention reduces the amount of trust between actors in the network. Since trust is an important factor in explaining satisfactory outcomes (see Klijn, Steijn et al. 2010), the reduction of trust by negative media attention also has negative effects on the outcomes.

5.4 BRANDING AS GOVERNANCE STRATEGY TO COPE WITH MEDIA

We have argued so far that, although branding is only in its infancy in gov-ernance processes, its importance is growing. One reason for that growth is the same as in the private sector: the fast-rising importance of the media as sources of information and for making sense of the world. Brands are a new way to communicate meaning in a media society (Arvidsson 2006); and this is not different for policymakers, public managers, and other actors in governance processes. They also need to communicate with the media and handle the media in complex decision-making processes. More and more actors in the public sector use brands to do that. In this section, we dis-cuss how branding works in mediatized governance processes. We discuss three main issues: firstly, how brands are used as instruments for commu-nication that accommodate certain characteristics of media. Secondly, we elaborate on how brands are used to frame projects and leaders. Thirdly, we discuss how brands are used to shield projects and leaders. Framing is a strategy that relies more on facilitating specific interpretations of events (front stage and backstage), whereas shielding refers more to a strategy of using a symbolic façade (front stage) to decrease people's desire to take a look backstage.

Brands as Instruments to Communicate with the Media

With the increasing importance of the media, it has become crucial in gov-ernance processes to communicate to the media the aims of the process, the ongoing development of the process, and the possible outcomes. Brands can be used to do this, because they have a number of characteristics that fit well in media society. Brands are symbols, and symbols are crucial to construct messages in the political spectacle (Edelman 1977; Fischer 2003). Thus brands connect well with the importance of the symbolic dimension of policymaking and the need to give meaning to complex governance processes in the media, not by extensively and rationally explaining policies, but by symbolizing essential aspects of them.

In modern media, there is a need to convey messages effectively in a short time, since one often has only a very limited time slot. This has to do with the standard formats of media, as explained in section 5.2. Branding fits with this because it uses heuristics (slogans and sound bites) rather than extensive discursive explanations that take a lot of time. Branding is based on evoking associations, and those can be triggered quickly in the media without providing great amounts of information. The visual element of branding is also apt. Visuals can be communicated in a relatively short time, and they easily trigger strong associations. Branding can thus be used to quickly convey a visual image of the idea behind a governance process. This connects well to the importance of the visual in media such as television and the Internet.

Branding can also be used to accommodate another development in the media landscape discussed earlier (see sections 5.2 and 5.3), namely dramatization. Dramatization requires the conveying of emotions, and this is exactly what brands do. Brands add emotional meaning to a branded object. They can be used to convey, for example, the empathy behind a certain policy, or the excitement in the case of an innovative project or an upcoming leader. Communicating emotions also helps to attract attention, as explained in Chapter 3. Attracting attention has always been important in the media, but maybe it has become even more important in the commercialized media environment where the media need to attract large audiences to make a profit.

Thus, in a number of ways, brands are adapted well to a mediatized environment. They probably fit better with the main characteristics of media logic than more classical policy instruments such as policy documents, political statements, or even modern interactive (deliberative) governance strategies. It is not very "sexy" to communicate to the media that you are organizing an interactive governance process and that you are going to manage that well. It is hard to communicate the deliberations in such a process in the media. It is simply too complicated and difficult to satisfy the need for a sound bite or to fill a short media "hole" in the 8 o'clock news. Brands, however, can be put in a short media format since they communicate both visuals and (emotional) associations very quickly. It is far easier to communicate the new policy proposals for a carbon neutral development of a new neighborhood with some good pictures and slogans about what to achieve, than by a thick report with all the background statistics.

Brands to Convey Identities and Images of Projects and Leaders

Brands provide images that can be used by political leaders and public managers to construct and communicate a particular identity and enhance the image of themselves as leaders. This connects well to the tendency of personalization in the media discussed in section 5.2. Brands can also be applied to construct identities and images of projects and policies, whereby they can brand the project both in terms of its content and in terms of its style (e.g. interactive or innovative). Using brands to convey identity and images has two important advantages. The first is that brands (if constructed in the right way) can be used for a longer period. By communicating a particular identity and particular images over a longer time, one can give governance projects and governance processes a certain continuity.

Despite the complexities, changing actors, and external events that might influence leaders, projects, or policies, the brand that symbolizes and represents the core idea and associations of the project or process remains more or less the same. That can be used to stress and communicate governance continuity and provide the project with a favorable image and associations that facilitate favorable media attention.

But brands can also provide leaders and projects with a certain image, and we have seen that image is crucial in the media society. In this regard, brands can construct and communicate image also in terms of style. This has the advantage that there is less need to communicate complex policy content in great detail. One can communicate a certain policy measure and use the brand to create associations with a particular style (for example, decisive, flamboyant, or innovative). If it concerns a leader, the communication of style helps to construct a personality and create (emotional) connections with the public. If it concerns a project, it helps to distinguish the project from other projects and facilitates certain interpretations of policy ideas in terms of the style (e.g. innovative). At this point, brands offer opportunities that most classical policy instrument do not. Brands provide leaders with instant associations of their performance and style that can be communicated more easily than complex explanations of policy theories and policy goals. In that sense, they also fit better with the characteristics of the drama democracy elaborated in sections 5.2 and 5.3.

Brands as Façades to Shield Governance Processes from the Media

Branding can also be applied to construct a façade or a visible exterior of a governance process. Such a façade plays a role in impression management in the sense that it gives the media (and other outsiders) particular impressions and images about the governance process. The façade of a governance process is what actors, such as journalists, see from outside. Branding is then applied to create a symbolic façade of, for example, websites, stylish policy documents, or pilot projects with images, logos, sound bites, and stories that communicate strategically chosen messages. If constructed well, the façade may not only facilitate certain interpretations of the governance process, but also play a role in shielding the governance process from the media (see also Van Twist 2009). As stated many times already, many governance processes are complex, and they take a lot of time because of the time-consuming interactions needed to arrive at package deals and solutions that generate enough support from various stakeholders to be implemented. This process is difficult to communicate to the media, since they want quick and clear results, dramatic and personalized stories. Thus governance processes are in an awkward position: they need time and dedication and some "invisibility" to facilitate interactions and negotiations between the involved actors; but media attention focuses mainly on the short term and on dramatizing conflict stories. This complicates matters in a governance context. Branding can then provide a façade of images, symbols, and stories that are easily available to outsiders. The façade provides the media with frames and basic information to use in their stories. The façade therefore helps to manage media attention and direct the media away from what is happening behind the façade. Of course, such a façade cannot keep the media away if they become really interested in what is going on behind the policy documents and websites, but in the daily practice of governance processes it can help to create room for maneuver behind the scenes. If properly constructed, the façade will provide the media with the information and images they need for their story.

Van Twist (2009) gives an example of constructing a façade for a minister of infrastructure who is filmed wearing a helmet and boots against the background of a construction site with a lot of sand and large trucks driving around. As Van Twist (2009) suggests, it is an example of celebrating the success that was created in a laborious and complex process behind the façade, by branding the process—and the minister—as examples of decisiveness and implementation power.

Let us return to the example of public–private partnerships (PPPs) as brands, as used in Chapter 4. The PPP brand provides projects with an image of efficiency and effectiveness. The idea of involving the private sector facilitates associations with efficiency, and the stress on effective collaborative forms strengthens the impression of leadership and decisiveness. However, Steijn et al. (2011) and Kort and Klijn (2011) show in two different surveys that the organizational form of PPPs is not significantly correlated with the achieved outcomes. The organizational form largely serves as a façade: it provides an exterior image of efficiency with a rhetorical story line that satisfies media, citizens, and other groups. But what is important to the outcomes is not the organizational form but the management practices behind the scenes (Steijn et al. 2011; Kort and Klijn 2011). Thus PPP provides a brand and an image for a project that is used to reassure everyone that what is done here is good. Then behind the scenes, everyone (and especially the professionals) can get on with their job: managing complex processes.

Of course there is a risk attached to using brands to construct façades and decors, because it may hinder transparency, and ultimately a lack of transparency is a threat to democracy. Whether branding constitutes a threat to transparency depends on such things as the kind and quality of information that the façade provides. In Chapter 7, we elaborate on the risks of branding.

Now it is important to note that the essence of the façade function of brands is not that it is useless. The fact that there is no impact on the outcomes of the organizational form of PPP and the brand story that goes with it—PPP is an efficient, arm's length organization that can do a good and swift job—does not mean that the brand is useless. As a communication instrument, the brand is useful because it creates momentum and support to do the job. In a media society, the image and the story line that come with a governance process are more important than ever, and a brand that constructs those fulfills a serious function.

5.5 CONCLUSION: BRANDS AS MODERN GOVERNANCE IN A MEDIATIZED WORLD

Public managers and politicians use brands to fulfill an important need of theirs, that is, to communicate with the media and provide clear images and motivating ideas to receive publicity. Brands can provide actors with symbols; this is important in the political spectacle (cf. Edelman 1988). The possibility of communicating emotional meaning through brands fits what Elchardus (2002) has termed the drama democracy. With brands, managers and politicians try to communicate a single message without having to explain all the details of the complex process. Needham (2006, 184) has argued that "successful leaders are those who are able to offer personalized brands, with simple, aspirational and consistent messages, built on a small number of symbolic policies rather than a broad legislative programme." At the same time, brands are applied to construct an image of the whole process and give it a certain continuity; this is crucial for long-lasting governance processes. In short, brands are used to frame and shield governance processes in relation to the media. Framing information through branding can also become a form of spinning information. This is one of the risks of branding that we elaborate in Chapter 7.

Finally, we wish to remark that, for brands to fulfill the role of constructing identity and giving continuity to governance processes, it is important that they are supported by many actors in the network. Consequently, the brand must be well anchored in the network where the complex governance process is taking place.

6   Branding as Governance Strategy

6.1   INTRODUCTION: BRANDING AS GOVERNANCE STRATEGY

In 1997, the Labour Party won the British elections by a landslide vote change (419 seats of the 650 available seats, 43 percent of the popular vote). Rebranding the Labour Party as "New Labour" and co-branding it with the "Third Way" brand, the party achieved a completely different image with the voters. The brand had been built in 1997 on the promise of change (new way of government) and new ideas for change as described in Chapters 1 and 2.

By 2005 however, the positive image had diminished considerably, and to win their third election in a row Labour needed to renew the brand. Voters considered the Conservatives as a good alternative. Building on the old brand, the Labour Party tried to extend the brand with new associations. Research had shown that the brand had become hollow and very much dependent on the leader, Tony Blair. The new associations that were made mainly focused not so much on promises, but on delivery of the promises made in the earlier campaigns. There was stress on what had been achieved and what still had to be achieved in the coming years (especially domestically). Labour was branded as "progressive realist," an image that fitted the idea of delivery (Lees-Marshment 2009). At the same time, Labour tried to strengthen the communication of the brand throughout the whole organization.

Blair succeeded where no Labour leader had succeeded before by winning his third election in a row, although Labour lost a lot of seats compared to the first two elections.

Brands Need Constant Nurturing and Management

The example of the rebranding of the Labour Party shows two things: (1) brand management is an important element in the management of political processes (The management of the Labour brand was an integral part of Labour's attempts to manage the elections); (2) brands can be, and are being, managed, but they need constant nurturing and can also be extended (see also Lees-Marshment 2009; Loken and Roedder John 2010).

Brands are constantly reinterpreted because they get meaning through consumers' and citizens' interpretations and because they are subject to external influences and change events. They have to be adjusted to new situations. This means that brands are not static and have to be managed constantly. Needham (2006, 181) states about branding political leaders and parties: "All political parties face the challenge of fostering an attractive brand, but there are distinctive challenges for incumbent parties. Incumbent parties are under pressure to sustain their winning coalition from within office in order to secure 'repeated purchases.' In a political terrain of declining party membership and voter de-alignment, successful candidates cannot assume that positive impressions that brought them to victory will keep their winning voter coalition together until the next election. They must build relationships with voters in order to secure positive endorsements, whereas opposition parties may be able to secure support simply through a policy of differentiation."

And this holds true not only for brands of political leaders and parties, but also for other brands in governance processes. Due to the non-linear dynamics caused by interactions between various actors, changing political, social, and natural contexts, as well as pressure from the media, it is important to actively maintain successful brands and renew them when the situation changes or the brand is no longer effective in the process. Thus, brand management in governance processes is crucial to maintain or even enhance the effectiveness of brands for the governance process. Consequently, brand management must take into account the characteristics of governance processes, i.e. the non-linear dynamics touched upon above, and also the multiplicity of actors and the interdependencies among them, as well as the ambiguities and varying insights about problems and solutions. The interdependencies among actors create situations in which it is very difficult for a single actor to realize a strong brand without the support of the others. This calls for brand management that includes all the actors with essential resources and that is geared towards getting their support for the brand. Given that the goal of branding is usually to create positive associations or gain support for a policy or a public service, it may be unwise to run the risk of triggering resistance and negative associations by not involving actors in the branding process. This risk is especially prevalent in public sectors where branding and marketing tools are viewed with a certain suspicion. With regard to the ambiguity in many governance processes, brand management needs to bridge different perceptions. This means that brands need to leave room for a certain degree of variety in meaning-making, instead of fixating its meaning to a detailed level, and severely narrowing its meaning.

Brand Management and Governance

In much of the governance literature, emphasis is laid on the managerial part of governance processes. Under the heading of network management, meta governance, process management, or other terms, strategies are described to facilitate and guide governance processes. Actually, one can safely say that these managerial strategies are considered just as important in the governance literature as they are in the branding literature: there is no success without adequate managerial effort. But although both bodies of literature agree on the importance of managerial effort and strategies, the actual strategies and activities they propose differ from one another in many respects. In this chapter, we delve into the way managerial branding strategies differ from those proposed for managing governance networks and processes, and what brand management can add to these. We look at the management of brands as a relatively new strategy for managing governance processes. As we shall see, brand management, although it can be used to generate support and stimulate interaction, is a governance strategy for managing perceptions and achieves other ends by starting with perceptions. By managing the brand, one tries to manage the development of ideas and perceptions in a certain community or network of stakeholders, and bind actors to the brand and to each other. The chapter is structured as follows. We start by discussing recent insights into how governance networks and governance processes are managed (section 6.2). Then we focus on the main differences between these types of strategies and brand management strategies (section 6.3). The chapter continues with an extensive treatment of the various managerial activities and strategies to manage brands (sections 6.4, 6.5, 6.6, 6.7, and 6.8). We end with conclusions about applying brand management strategies in governance (section 6.9).

6.2   MANAGING GOVERNANCE NETWORKS: THE STATE OF THE ART

Classical top-down ways of steering—especially by judicial instruments, subsidies, or other more unilateral ways of governing—have been criticized widely for not being effective in governance networks where governments are more or less dependent on a wide variety of other actors (see e.g. Kickert et al. 1997; Sørensen and Torfing 2007; Teisman et al. 2009). Thus there has been a search for new managerial strategies to manage governance networks. This is generally referred to as network management.

What Is Managing Governance Networks About?

Since cooperation and the coordination of goals and interests in governance networks, and the processes within these networks, do not occur of their own accord, it is necessary to steer interactions in policy games within networks. Network management is a deliberate attempt to govern processes in networks. Network management aims to initiate and facilitate interaction processes between actors (Friend et al. 1974), creating and changing network arrangements for better coordination (Scharpf 1978; Rogers and Whetten 1982), and, for instance, creating new content by exploring new ideas (Koppenjan and Klijn 2004) as well as guiding interactions (Gage and Mandell 1990; Kickert et al. 1997).

The implicit assumption in most of the literature is that a satisfactory outcome is often impossible without management of governance networks (Gage and Mandell 1990; Kickert et al. 1997; Agranoff and McGuire 2001). Various management strategies have been identified in the literature. In general, most of these network management strategies can be categorized as strategies of process management or institutional design (Gage and Mandell 1990; Koppenjan and Klijn 2004). Process management strategies attempt to facilitate interactions between actors in policy games in networks. What is crucial in these types of strategies is that, although they are indirect in the sense that they try to facilitate interactions and the actions of other actors, they take the structure of the network (the rules, positions of actors, and resource division) as a given. Because they are strategies that focus on actors and interactions, they are hands-on strategies (see also: Sørensen and Torfing 2007). If management strategies are aimed at altering the institutional characteristics of the network (such as changing actor positions or entry rules), they can be labeled as institutional design strategies (Koppenjan and Klijn 2004).

Strategies for the Management of Governance Networks

The number of network management strategies identified in the literature is impressive, and this is not the place to describe them all (see Gage and Mandell 1990; O'Toole 1988; Agranoff and McGuire 2001; or, for an extensive overview, Koppenjan and Klijn 2004). It is clear, however, that if the network manager is to achieve important outcomes a range of different strategies is required (see Kickert et al. 1997; Agranoff and McGuire 2001): activating actors and resources, coordinating goal-achieving mechanisms (including influencing the perceptions and goals of other actors), fostering organizational arrangements to facilitate and enable interactions between actors, and coordinating the stream of actions and interactions between different actors.

On the other hand, we have seen that networks consist of concrete interactions between actors within a network structure that is created by the actors (partly willingly and consciously, but also partly as a result of prior interactions and established ways of behaving). This means that network management strategies can be aimed at either bringing about changes in the interactions of actors, or effecting changes at the network level, or both (Kickert et al. 1997).

Although making no claims to be exhaustive, Table 6.1 summarizes the main network management strategies (for an overview of the many different network management strategies: Hanf and Scharpf 1978; O'Toole

Table 6.1   Overview of Network Management Strategies

	Activation of Actors and Resources	Goal-Achieving Strategies	Organizational Arrangements	Interaction Guiding
Management of interactions	Selective activation, resource mobilization, stabilization, deactivation of actors and resources, initiating new series of interaction, coalition building	Searching for goal congruency, creating variation in solutions, influencing (and explicating) perceptions, managing and collecting information and research	Creating new ad hoc organizational arrangements (boards, project organizations, etc.)	Mediation, brokerage, appointing process manager, removing obstacles to cooperation, creating incentives for cooperation
Management of network	Network activation, changing composition of networks, changing position of actors	Reframing of perceptions, changing decision rules in networks, changing information flow permanently	Creating permanent organizational constructions	Changing or setting rules for conflict regulation, for information flow, changing pay-off rules or professional codes

Source: Adapted from Klijn (2005).

1988; Gage and Mandell 1990; Kickert et al. 1997; Agranoff and McGuire 2001; Koppenjan and Klijn 2004). Not all the strategies mentioned in any one cell are mutually exclusive. One can, for instance, influence the perceptions of actors by initiating a search process for a variety in solutions.

Strategies for the activation of actors or resources are useful to initiate governance processes. The network manager has to identify the actors necessary for an initiative and actually create a situation in which they become interested in investing their resources (see also Lynn 1981). Scharpf (1978) calls this selective activation: correct identification of necessary participants and a lack of opposition from other actors with the ability to block the initiative are crucial for inter-organizational governance processes. Conversely, the manager may wish to deactivate actors if their involvement is not productive. This of course also evokes normative questions that unfortunately require space that is not available in this chapter. Once the process has started, it is necessary to clarify the goals and perceptions of actors and to try to invest time and money in developing solutions that create opportunities for actors' participation (Koppenjan and Klijn 2004). However, creating temporary organizational arrangements to facilitate interactions is also important (Mulford and Rogers 1982; Gage and Mandell 1990).

Of course, the transaction costs of these arrangements have to be kept as low as possible. Most of the time actors themselves understand this very well. Despite all the talk about coordinating partnerships however, empirical research shows that often organizational arrangements are lacking or relatively light (Osborne 2000; Hodge and Greve 2005; Steijn et al. 2011). And last but not least, the interactions in the game itself have to be managed. This can be done by appointing a process manager who invests time and energy in connecting the actions and strategies of actors to each other during the interactions.

At the network level, the manager also has opportunities to intervene. Contrary to strategies that aim at managing the interactions, that take the network (and its rules and beliefs) as given, these strategies are aimed at changing the network mostly by changing rules in the network. These could be rules on entry and exit (allowing new actors to enter), rules on evaluation (for instance in a very classical way by changing the reward structure by means of subsidizing), or changing conflict rules (for an extensive elaboration of various strategies, see Koppenjan and Klijn 2004).

Managing Governance Networks: Necessary but Time Consuming

Governance networks need to be managed, most importantly, because of the complexity of policymaking and service delivery since, in order to achieve worthwhile results, a wide variety of actors and policy levels have to be connected. As Agranoff and McGuire (2003, 123) conclude in their study on how city officials work with other layers of government and organizations to develop their city economics: "From the perspective of the city government, there is not one cluster of linkages to manage but several clusters—some horizontal, some vertical, and some that include both within a context of a single project or program."

Thus network management is strongly related to achieving good outcomes in governance processes as is shown by a lot of research on the effect of network management. In many case studies on governance networks, network management strategies have been shown to play a prominent role and are said to be crucial for achieving good results (Huang and Provan 2007; Meier and O'Toole 2007; Klijn, Edelenbos et al. 2010). Edelenbos and Klijn (2006, 436), after comparing six interactive decision-making cases, concluded that: "Our findings on these six case studies do, however, provide a good impression of the importance of good process management for the success of interactive decision-making processes. Management matters in the successful evolution of interactive decision-making processes."

And this relation between network management strategies and outcomes is confirmed by several survey research studies on network management and outcomes of governance networks. Huang and Provan (2007) have shown that network involvement, or network embeddedness, is positively related to social outcomes. Meier and O'Toole (2001, 2007), in their well-known studies on educational districts in Texas, have shown that network-ing by district managers is positively correlated with the performance of the district. Klijn, Edelenbos et al. (2010) showed that the number of employed network management strategies correlates strongly to outcomes as per-ceived by the respondents.

Network management strategies are extremely time consuming. Since networks and the complex governance processes within them need constant nurturing and many managerial efforts, an active organization is required to do the job. In many cases this is a governmental organization, but it can also be a non-governmental organization.

Network Management Compared to Branding

If we look at the network management literature, we see that network man-agement is very much focused on making connections and facilitating inter-actions. Insofar as network management aims to influence perceptions, it does so in an indirect way, mainly by organizing interactions between actors in which ideas can be exchanged and discussed. Branding strategies are primarily about the management of perceptions. The management of interactions and relationships is secondary to that in branding. In the next section, we elaborate on the similarities and differences of the two types of strategies more in depth.

6.3   HOW BRANDING DIFFERS FROM MANAGING GOVERNANCE NETWORKS AND FROM PROCESSES

Throughout this book, we have paid attention to differences between branding and more classical approaches to governance processes in pub-lic administration. If we compare brand management with network man-agement, we observe several differences. Table 6.2 summarizes some of the main differences between branding and the management of gover-nance networks.

The first difference relates to the view on governance and governance processes. Although the branding literature rarely states explicit assump-tions about governance, we can find ideas about influencing decision-making processes. The governance literature tends to aim primarily at governance structures and interactions among actors, whereas branding is directly aimed at perceptions and ideas.

A basic assumption in the branding literature is that one can create loy-alty (repeated purchases in terms of products or repeated support for gov-ernance ideas) by creating strong images with associations. So governance through brand management is aimed at creating long-lasting loyalties by means of associations and emotions. In governance processes, the stress is more on creating loyalties by facilitating interactions among actors.

Table 6.2 Differences between Branding Strategies and Network Management Strategies

	Network Management Strategies	Branding Strategies
Governance assumptions and puzzles	Governance processes are difficult to manage because of various (conflicting) perceptions, interests, and strategies. Also, problems cut through governmental layers and institutional jurisdictions. This causes complexity that has to be handled by making new connections between actors, ideas, and interactions.	Governance processes are difficult to manage because actors have considerable autonomy on the one hand and their attention has to be attracted in a mediatized world with many competing images and loyalties, making it difficult to reach actors/consumers. This has to be handled by creating strong brands that can communicate with, and get the attention of, actors.
Emphasis (how to influence actors' behavior)	Bind actors with horizontal relations through increasing connections, creating joint conditions for information exchange, enhancing trust relations and the flow of information to find promising solutions	Influence perceptions by adding meaning to branded objects with visual images and appeal to emotions
Types of strategies	• Activating actors (mobilize them) • Connecting and arranging (increase connections) • Exploring content/connecting frames and goals • Setting process rules for inter-actions	• Market research; searching for information and determining target groups • Brand construction; developing associations and carriers for the brand • Communicating brands; reaching target groups and generating support • Brand maintenance; adapting, defending, and reproducing the brand
Limitations	• Urgency and interdependencies between actors crucial. Without the two, it is difficult for network management strategies to succeed • Network management is hard work and requires great skills • Limited control of actors' actions, therefore outcomes unpredictable and sometimes doubt about the effects	• Building strong images and associations does not secure actions and "getting things done" (action gap) • Brands can be counter branded or challenged

Thus we can conclude that governance networks management and branding differ in their primary focus and emphasis. Network management strategies strongly emphasize that actors can be bound by horizontal connecting strategies and increasing interactions, information, and trust between actors in the governance network. Branding emphasizes more that actors can be bound by strong images and appeal to emotions. Although both approaches give attention to constructing ideas, aligning actors' perceptions, and creating variations in ideas by providing new images, branding has a much stronger symbolic character than network management, which relies more on classic strategies like generating information, creating scenarios, and so on, and this is reflected in the types of strategies deployed, as can be seen in Table 6.2.

Both approaches to managing governance processes have their limitations and weak spots. The limitation of network management strategies clearly is the need for urgency and interdependence, whereas the weak point of branding strategies—which rely heavily on influencing actors' way of looking at and appreciating the brand—is that it is not certain that this really will result in actual actions. This is certainly not insignificant as most governance processes require a lot of coordinating and joint action for anything to happen. It is one thing to achieve repeated sales of a product—requiring a relatively simple act on the part of a consumer—but it is quite another thing to realize repeated deliberate joint action between various actors simultaneously in a governance process. Thus although brands may be able to bind actors to an idea and influence perceptions of problems and solutions in the governance network, this is probably not sufficient to arrive at joint governance. It also requires coordination activities that have been described widely in the literature on managing governance networks.

In that sense, the management of governance networks by directly facilitating and stimulating interactions on the one hand, and brand management on the other hand, can be seen as complements rather than substitutes. It is unlikely that branding can replace network management as a managerial strategy in governance processes. It is more likely that branding will be used as an additional strategy to manage governance processes because it can contribute something most of the network management strategies do not have. Thus we will probably see mangers using branding strategies alongside network management strategies in governance processes. We have already discussed the network management strategies that managers can employ. The next section deals extensively with the most important branding strategies that can be employed.

6.4   MANAGING BRANDS IN GOVERNANCE PROCESSES: STRATEGIES AND ORIENTATIONS

Now it is clear that brands do not emerge or develop automatically. The literature emphasizes that product development and branding are often complex and that many uncertainties are attached to the whole process of creating and managing a brand (e.g. Lees-Marshment 2009; Blichfeldt 2005). As we saw in section 6.1, brands have to be created, worked out, communicated, adapted, and defended. Thus branding requires a lot of managerial activities to actually happen. In this section, we lay out various strategies for brand management that can be applied in the management of governance processes.

What Kinds of Strategies Are Involved in Branding?

The literature on brand management and branding strategies is extremely elaborate. Thus it may come as no surprise that a multitude of branding strategies and management activities have been described and analyzed. Strategies vary from classical ones such as the designing of a suitable logo and slogan, to managing touch points with consumers, and doing ethnographic research among target groups to understand their needs. Only part of each strategy is aimed directly at creating the brand. It has been stressed time and again in the literature that market research on various opinions of target groups is important (see e.g. Kotler et al. 1999; Kotler and Keller 2009). The city marketing literature stresses the importance of knowing what different target groups look for in a city (Braun 2008). The political marketing literature also mentions the importance of knowing what the target group values and appreciates when brands are being constructed (see Needham 2006; Lees-Marshment 2009). Both of these literature streams stress that creating the brand and communicating it is not only about developing a brand from the perspective of the brand owner (the political party). It is also about looking at voters' needs, their preferences and emotions, and molding the brand to that information (Lees-Marshment 2009). Thus in that vision, branding is also about exploring ideas and emotions among the target groups to improve the brand construction. The literature on political marketing and branding also stresses that brands need continuous improvement and have to be sustained to be effective since situations where the brand is used change, preferences change, and competitors are also trying to position themselves (Needham 2006). Sustainment of brands is also stressed in the literature on brand communities (Muniz and O'Guinn 2001; Arvidsson 2006), because this literature stresses that brands are produced and reproduced in dynamic social interaction between members of a community. Recently, more attention is also being given to defending brands against counter-branding activities or other actions of actors or media that threaten the brand (Loken et al. 2010). This means that managerial activity in branding is expanding and now consists of not only creating the brand and communicating it but also nurturing, changing, and defending it. Taking into account the variety of activities, we distinguish four categories of strategies:

- Market research. The aim is to gain information and understanding about preferences and needs of various stakeholders or target groups in governance processes. This aspect includes, for example, exploring opinions and emotions with the target groups, or determining the values they consider important, since the brand to be created must take those values into account. For instance in the case of policy ideas, market research may seek to ascertain the opinions and feelings of stakeholders and citizens on a particular issue or policy. One could say that in general market research has lots of elements in common with what has been termed stakeholder analysis or network analysis: exploring who the stakeholders are and what their relations are, identifying their perceptions and the differences in their perceptions (about values, policy problems, policy proposals, see Koppenjan and Klijn 2004).
- Brand construction and product development. This focuses on the development and building of the brand, which includes for example the development of brand values, as well as brand elements including symbols and images that represent the brand. In short, it involves the construction and development of the main brand characteristics. The strategy of brand construction is about developing a brand that symbolizes certain values and triggers the right associations among stakeholders and the wider public of governance processes. The aim is to direct stakeholder perceptions about policy problems and policy content, and bind them to the brand. Brand construction is largely a creative process. The construction of the brand cannot be decoupled from the development of the products to which the brand refers, for example a public service, a public policy, or a coalition of actors that promote certain policy initiatives. Because the characteristics of the product influence the perception of the brand, it is important to manage product development. This includes product design, product delivery, implementation, and so forth.
- Brand communication. The brand needs to be brought to the attention of the public in general and specific target groups or stakeholders in particular. After all, the brand has to fulfill a function both for the involved stakeholders and—as we have seen in Chapter 5—for the outside world and the media. This may include for example public relations, using all kinds of publicity and social media. Brand communication can be an element of managing governance processes because it may facilitate interaction with stakeholders through the brand. The aim is to communicate particular values and ideas, and enhance support.
- Brand maintenance and reproduction. Brands need nurturing in order to remain strong and endure over time. This is especially the case in the dynamic world of governance where we witness unexpected and non-linear developments. Governance processes are very susceptible

to changes in the political and societal environment. Policy issues may be very popular at one moment, and suddenly become unpopular the next. Thus the brand must be kept up to date. Maintenance and reproduction of a brand include sustaining, evaluating, and renewing the brand in order to adapt it to changing situations and shifting perceptions among stakeholders. It also involves protecting the brand, for example in the case of counter branding or illegitimate use of the brand. Brand maintenance is an attempt to manage the interpretations of brands and take protective measures against counter branding or brand dilutions. The strategy of brand maintenance and reproduction is to make sure that the brand fits and remains effective in a changing governance environment.

6.5   MARKET RESEARCH: SETTING THE STAGE FOR EFFECTIVE BRANDS

One of the first activities consists of doing market research into the ideas, beliefs, and emotions of possible stakeholders and target groups (Kotler et al. 1999; Braun 2008). This can be done of course in several ways and with different aims. If one takes an instrumental approach to branding—which starts from an existing policy or service and uses branding to persuade stakeholders of its qualities as we explained in Chapter 2—market research is applied to discover how the brand can be sold more effectively. Market research aims to discover how the target group can best be reached, and what images and emotions may persuade citizens; but if one takes a more horizontal approach to branding, then market research starts from the views and ideas of target groups. The question then is how target groups experience policy issues and governance ideas. How can their perceptions be used to create or improve the brand? If one sees the brand as a relationship with citizens, stakeholders, or particular target groups, thus if a more interactive approach to branding is used, then the market research question is more about how to secure the loyalty of the target group to the brand. In this case, market research focuses on the question of what people's relationship with the brand means to them, and what makes people loyal to the brand. In each case, market research takes a different direction and has to answer different questions, but, whatever perspective one chooses, knowledge about the views of targets groups is important because it provides information about the way stakeholders perceive certain ideas or governance aims, and this is crucial for constructing, communicating, and maintaining the brand.

Activities in Market Research

There is a wide variety of methods to conduct market research and obtain information about the beliefs and ideas of stakeholders and targets groups.

Mentality milieus in the Netherlands

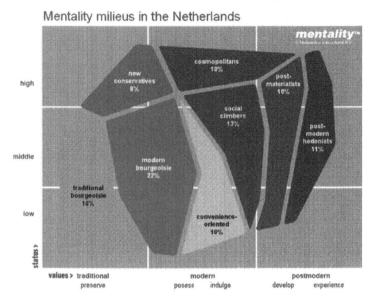

Figure 6.1   Segmentation of society in subgroups according to mentality.

Box 6.1   Motivaction Example of Various Groups in Society

Various lifestyle research agencies stress that modern societies are com-posed of different subgroups with different beliefs. The research bureau Motivaction (see http://www.motivaction.nl/specialismen/mentality-tm) has produced one such configuration (see Figure 6.1).

The idea presented assumes that groups of people in society can be divided by the nature of their values (modern/postmodern, linked to issues of lifestyle, family life, and so on) and their socio-demographic status (education and profession). This segmentation of society enables one to look at various reactions of various subgroups to policy proposals and at trends and where they emerge. On the basis of this segmentation, insights are acquired as to how groups will react to brands or proposals, which brands would be appreciated by which subgroups. Often, spe-cific market research is carried out for this, where various people are confronted with policy proposals or brands, or where brands are tested against competing brands.

Regular survey research can give indications of citizens' beliefs, and changes in beliefs. Sometimes, general surveys can be used, but often we need research on specific target groups since societies are segmented and each segment of society may need to be addressed in a different way. This certainly holds if policy measures are specifically aimed at a particular region or target group.

For example, in the case of policies for creating extra space for water storage in times of excessive rainfall in a particular region, the policy initiators need to know the preferences of specific groups in an area (nature conservationists, farmers, residents) to be able to construct a brand that fits with the ideas of important target groups. There are various segmentation options based on demarcations such as geographic, behavioral, demographic, or psychological characteristics (Lees-Marshment 2009). Using demarcation criteria results in the identification of various groups, on the assumption that these groups act differently when confronted with brands or marketing activities. Box 6.1 gives an indication of how a society might be segmented and how this affects brands and communicating brands.

In addition to survey research, information about targets groups may also be gathered by interviews and focus groups, for example by interviewing party members who are in close contact with voters, or by consulting specialists. Focus groups can provide specific information on people that are important for a governance process. Focus groups can include, for instance, citizens that voted for the party last time but are hesitant to do so now, or farmers that live in an area where water storage areas have to be developed; but focus groups can also be composed of citizens living in an urban regeneration area. Such focus groups can be useful to get a feel for the community in that area and how they view their area. This may generate information about how they feel about perceived problems and suggested solutions in the area, what they prioritize, and thus what brand characteristics would appeal to them. Moreover, focus groups can be integrated within other network management strategies discussed earlier. The focus group for instance could also be part of an interactive process to generate support. It then serves two purposes at the same time: generation of information about values and beliefs of stakeholders and generation of support by involving them in the process. In that way, brand management and network management strategies become integrated.

More recently, ethnographic research has been applied in market research, especially to analyze meaning-making in brand communities and in relationships between individuals and brands. Members of a brand community can be great sources of feedback information. They are inclined to use voice instead of exit because of their loyalty, and they are likely to be constructive rather than purely negative (Heding et al. 2009). Market research in communities should be unobtrusive. A heavy presence of marketing managers in brand communities may destroy the feeling of community (see e.g. Heding et al. 2009). The instrumental nature of a relationship between a professional marketer and members of a brand community possibly runs contrary to what people are seeking in the community. Ethnographic research therefore often involves participant observation; the researcher gathers data in a rather unobtrusive way by taking part in his research subjects' activities in order to understand what the brand means to them in their daily work and daily lives.

6.6   BRAND CONSTRUCTION AND PRODUCT DEVELOPMENT: MANAGING THE IMAGE

Of course, some of the most important managerial activities in brand management relate to creating the brand and developing the product that belongs to the brand. Brand construction firstly requires an idea of the main messages and associations that the brand wants to evoke. What is the brand identity; what are the main brand values to be developed? Brand construction also involves selecting the brand elements such as names, wordmarks, logos, slogans, and visual images, and it may involve the development of important carriers of the brand such as products, packages, celebrities, leaders, buildings, or the entire organization. In several governance processes, it may be relevant to consider the organization as a carrier of the brand. The reputation of the organization behind a program or a policy often influences the perception of that program or policy. For example, the perception of projects carried out by a state forestry organization is likely to be influenced by the image of the state forestry organization. If one takes this into account, then the brand owner may want to undertake activities to improve the brand of the organization. Brand management will then become more related to organizational development and take place at a strategic level in the organization (see also Heding et al. 2009).

An important goal during the construction of the brand is brand equity, which refers to the value of the brand to target groups. Brand equity is based on brand attributes and brand benefits. An example of brand attributes is the spatial appearance of a city in the case of city branding. Three types of brand benefits are important to consider during the construction of the brand:

1. *Functional* benefits: for example in the case of nature conservation policies the functional benefits for nature organizations or other stakeholders may be financial support through subsidies.
2. *Experiential* benefits: these are coupled to the sensory experience of using the brand, for example the pleasure of hiking through a nature conservation area.
3. *Symbolic* benefits: these contribute to self-expression, for example what participation in a successfully branded policy process means for the self-expression of a citizen or civil servant (cf. Heding et al. 2009).

All of the activities around the construction of the brand can either be based on the preferences of a (single) brand owner (instrumental branding), or be carried out in interaction with stakeholders (interactive branding) (see Chapter 3). In the context of governance processes, the brand manager should take into account that multiple actors may want to influence the brand and co-construct the brand (De Chernatony and Dall'Olmo Riley 1998). For example, in the case of a project that is being branded, the diverse partners in the project

Table 6.3 Levels of Participation in Brand Construction

Level of Participation	Stakeholders as	Management Strategy	Management Activities
Informing	Recipients of information	Brand manager takes decisions regarding the substance and process of branding, and informs other actors	Taking decisions about the brand
Consulting	Informants	Brand manager largely decides upon the brand, but regards other stakeholders as useful discussion partners	Organizing market research, facilitating discussion with stakeholders, taking decisions about the brand
Advising	Advisors who bring in ideas, raise problems, and formulate solutions	In principle, brand manager decides upon the brand but other actors play a fully fledged role in development of brand	Facilitating discussion with stakeholders, taking decisions about the brand
Co-decision	Co-deciders who bring in ideas and take responsibility for brand development	Stakeholders jointly decide upon the brand	Facilitating discussion and decision-making processes with stakeholders
Co-decision and co-production	Developers and producers of the brand	Brand manager leaves decision making about brand and production of the brand to stakeholders, and civil service plays an advisory role	Facilitating activities of networks and communities of stakeholders. Facilitating their decision making and creating the context for brand development

Source: Adapted from Arnstein 1971; Edelenbos 2000; Edelenbos and Klijn 2006.

or the target groups may want to be involved in the construction of the brand. The brand manager needs to decide the degree to which he wants to involve stakeholders in the construction of the brand (see Table 6.3). This is not the place to discuss the pros and cons of citizen participation in depth, because this has already been done extensively in the literature on stakeholder involvement and participation in governance (see e.g. Bekkers et al. 2007; Edelenbos 2005; Edelenbos and Klijn 2006; Mandell 2001; Van Buuren and Loorbach

2009). However, we do not wish to leave the main dilemma unaddressed. Involving stakeholders in the construction of the brand may complicate the construction of the brand, because it involves a lot of coordination and discussion among multiple actors. However, if stakeholders are ignored during the construction of the brand, chances are that they will give their own meaning to the brand after it has been introduced and communicate about the brand in ways that run contrary to the intention of the brand manager. In other words, non-participating stakeholders may reconstruct the brand in their own way after the brand manager has introduced the brand.

Table 6.3 shows that stakeholders can participate to different degrees in the construction of brands. The lowest level of participation is when stakeholders are informed about the content of the brand and the process of branding only after the decisions about the brand have been taken by the brand owner. This is instrumental branding. Branding becomes more interactive when stakeholders are involved as informants, advisors, or co-deciders. The strongest form of stakeholder participation is when stakeholders co-decide and co-produce the brand; they take most of the decisions about the brand, and they produce the brand during their activities in their networks and communities. An example of this is a social movement in which different stakeholders play a role. The brand is not developed by a brand manager but rather produced during the activities of the social movement. A community in a particular area may produce a community brand in a similar way. The municipality therefore plays only a role in facilitating particular communal activities, paying for a community center and for the maintenance of the public space outside in which the brand actually develops.

Especially if there is an active brand community (see Chapters 3 and 4), the brand manager may choose a role that is more about facilitating the activities of the community than about creating a brand himself. The brand is being constructed in and through the activities of the community. The advantage of this (from the brand manager's perspective) is that the brand is present in community activities and thus enters the personal or professional lives of the community members. As Arvidsson (2006, 90) has stressed, the value of a brand is "based on the ability to make the brand enter into social life and become an aspect of the relations, identities, fantasies, desires and hopes that social life generates." A disadvantage may be that the brand manager can exert only limited influence on how the brand is constructed because it is constructed by the community members in their culturally embedded stories and rituals. In summary, the brand manager needs to decide whether and to what extent he wants to construct the brand in his own organization or in the network/community. The greater the emphasis on the latter, the more the construction of the brand becomes a matter of managing the network of actors who co-construct the brand. In this case also, brand management becomes integrated with network management strategies. Box 6.2 illustrates the co-construction of a place brand by a municipality, a housing association, a developer, and residents.

Box 6.2   Branding a Community: Constructing an Appropriate Brand

Katendrecht is a community in Rotterdam (the Netherlands) largely surrounded by water. At the end of the nineteenth century, it was an important harbor zone. When the harbor moved westwards in the 1960s, the community started to decline and a negative image of the area developed. Criminality became clearly visible. Currently, the area is being regenerated. About 1,600 new residences have been built along the waterfront, and the old town center has been renovated. To attract new residents and entrepreneurs, a campaign was launched to rebrand the community.

The campaign, with the motto Can You Handle the Cape (see www. kunjijdekaapaan.nl), does not ignore the character of the community. It mentions that the place is perceived to be dangerous, and then adds a twist of adventure. The campaign is full of symbolism and refers to sea-faring, water, and adventure. The community is presented as a unique place with slightly eccentric residents (see Figure 6.2). It does not aim to explain the community's qualities with fact sheets. Instead, it communicates what the community feels like, conveying a feeling of distinctiveness, character, and adventure. Thus, it is portrayed as the opposite of a dull or middle-of-the-road community.

What is important in terms of public management is how the campaign was developed and how the brand evolved after the campaign was launched. The branding campaign was a co-production between the city council, the district council, the main developer, the housing association, and a citizens' organization. The housing association and the main developer were involved because they had a stake in the brand and because their communications influenced the brand. If they had not been involved in the branding process, their communications might have gone against the brand. One of the reasons that the citizens' group participated was that they seemed well connected in the community and they had influence among the local residents. It therefore mattered whether the citizens' group supported or did not support the brand. Their opposition to the campaign would have been a major setback.

The citizens' group actively influenced the branding campaign so as to prevent the brand from portraying an idealized picture that targeted only the upper-middle class from outside the community. The citizens' group was interested in a brand that reflected and strengthened what the residents appreciated in their community, instead of an over-the-top branding campaign that promised the world and neglected the existing character of the community. The discussions about the brand entailed political arguments and choices about what kind of community to develop (policy goals). It was agreed that the brand needed to reflect a balance between renewal in the community (as evidenced by the demolition of   *Continued* old houses and the building of new apartments) and renovating and preserving the existing community (supported by renovating the old center). Also, the parties sought to create a brand that reflected a mix of income and ethnicities. The discussions with the citizens' group concerned not only the basic message and idea of the branding campaign, but also the choice of images, slogans, and logos.

The interactive part of the branding campaign was not restricted to interacting with the citizens' group (indirect citizen participation), but also included a limited form of direct participation. There was one interactive session about the brand with about 20 people who worked or lived in the community. This session was meant to determine the brand values that would underlie the campaign. The brand values were determined by discussing and drawing the current identity of the community and its aspired identity. The branding expert who organized and facilitated the interactive session with the citizens used the input from the session to develop a narrative about the community. This was discussed with the citizens and then a marketing bureau was hired to develop a branding campaign (including images, slogans, and a logo) on the basis of all input. The concepts developed by the marketing bureau were discussed with the main stakeholders, including the citizens' association.

Figure 6.2   Image entitled "A cozy chat with the neighbor" from the branding campaign in Katendrecht.

Managerial Activities in the Construction of the Brand

The construction of a brand is a process that does not come about by itself. It needs to be managed actively. As elaborated in Chapter 2, brand construction involves activities like creating a logo, a slogan, and a strong visual image; but that is only the technical aspect of brand creation. In general, brands are about evoking associations. In this section, we discuss two main categories of activities that brand managers can employ to enhance the development and evocation of associations with the brand. Firstly, the brand manager can facilitate decision-making processes in which professionals and target groups discuss and decide on the associations that a brand should trigger. Secondly, the manager can manage the processes of brand construction that take place among the users of the brand (during the use or "consumption" of the brand). The brand manager can create events and environments where the brand can be experienced and lived out. In this way, he can influence the context in which the brand is being used or consumed, and thus influence the experience of the brand and the position of the brand (without directly communicating particular ideas or associations). We will come back to this strategy further on.

With regard to the associations that the brand aims to trigger, a main consideration is of course the core identity and the main message of the brand. For example, a particular policy to stimulate investments in solar energy can be branded as a policy that stimulates innovation, entrepreneurship, and highly skilled employment, or it can be branded around sustainability and caring for the future of our children. The core identity of a brand may be determined by thinking in terms of the aspired brand values. Examples of brand values include honesty, equality, or fun. Also, it is important to construct the brand identity at an emotional level. What feelings and emotions does the brand want to evoke? Whatever associations the parties involved want to evoke with the brand, the associations should have a certain level of congruence. If the associations are not congruent enough, stakeholders will not understand the brand easily, the different associations may not be connected in the brain, and therefore the image of the brand may remain incomplete or weak. This may also limit the recognition and recollection of the brand. Further, the associations that one wants to trigger need to be favorable, strong, and unique (Heding et al. 2009). Of course, unique associations are important to distinguish the brand from competitors and develop unique selling points. Choosing unique associations may therefore also include an analysis of competitors. For a brand to be favorable, one needs to connect to stakeholder preferences. In a governance context, it may not be easy to construct a brand that is favored by all actors, since some of the actors may have opposing interests and views. One way of dealing with this may be to involve the stakeholders in the construction of the brand in order to let them clarify what they want and try to integrate their wishes. The brand manager needs to take into account, however, that giving all wishes a place in the brand may lead to so many concessions that one is left with a flavorless brand that fails to create any enthusiasm. Such a brand may also fail to trigger any strong associations, or associations that appear quickly in the minds of stakeholders and demand attention (Heding et al. 2009). However, it is certainly not impossible to create a brand that gains the support of all stakeholders. Good and original ideas for brands may still capture the imagination and enthusiasm of everyone involved. It is even possible for a well-chosen brand to contribute to overcoming problems and tensions between stakeholders.

Given the importance of a brand being supported by multiple stakeholders in the network, brand management may involve the development of the message and the brand associations interactively with the network of stakeholders. As indicated in Table 6.3, stakeholder involvement may differ from consulting stakeholders to seeing stakeholders as the main decision makers and producers of the brand. If brand managers choose more intensive forms of stakeholder involvement, then it is important to facilitate interaction with stakeholders and coordinate joint learning processes in order to mobilize and direct the energies and enthusiasm of the network. In fact, the brand manager draws on the network management strategies described in section 6.2. Network management strategies then become part of the strategy for developing a brand, but conversely the joint development of a brand can be part of network management; the process of joint brand development may serve to increase interaction and strengthen relationships among the actors in the network.

Apart from facilitating decision making about the brand and its associations, brand management is also about creating opportunities for other stakeholders to make the brand come true. One of the things that brand managers can do is facilitate environments and events where the brand can be developed and lived out. For example, the development of a community brand or a city brand can be facilitated by organizing events and festivities wherein the brand can be lived and developed. The brand of a political party or organization can also be strengthened by organizing events where the members of the party or organization come together and live out the brand. This may be important, for example, if some of the brand messages have to do with "liveliness" or "sociability." The brand manager focuses on choosing and creating a particular surrounding, with particular participants and a particular program where the brand is present (or actively presented). The atmosphere and context of the event then influences how the brand is perceived and the meaning ascribed to it.

Some considerations in relation to the facilitation of events include the kind of events that are facilitated (for example a dance for teenagers strengthens particular associations, whereas facilitating an open-air classical concert or a fun fair strengthens somewhat different associations), the environment in which they take place (for example an up-market conference center, a farm, a castle, or a common pub), and the way in which brand elements are brought to people's attention, made visible, and positioned.

Consequently, the brand elements should be visible not only to the people who participate in the event, but also to those who see the event through the media.

In some cases, the brand manager may even focus on the event as a media event, as for example was the case with the landing of former U.S. president George W. Bush on the deck of the aircraft carrier USS *Abraham Lincoln*, described in Chapter 3 (see Figure 6.3). The people participating in such events then become less important as active constructers of the brand; they become more like "human wallpaper" that functions to position the (branded) leader as somebody who is among the people (see Figures 6.3 and 6.4). Of course this raises ethical issues that have to be considered. We deal with ethical issues around branding more elaborately in Chapter 7.

In place branding and political branding in particular, the organization of events to enhance visibility of the brand is a well-known strategy. It can involve cultural events but also interactive meetings and hearings with various stakeholders. Actually here, classical and modern forms of communicating policy come together. The main difference is that classical hearings and meetings tend to put the exchange of arguments and information center stage, whereas other events work more from the assumption that stakeholders and target groups should engage, co-create, and enjoy the brand. The brand experience and reproduction of the brand by experiencing it in a certain context are given more attention than in classical governance management strategies.

Figure 6.3   George W. Bush announcing U.S. victory on aircraft carrier with main message (mission accomplished) and military personnel in the background. Source: Associated Press (AP).

Figure 6.4   French president Sarkozy delivers speech with workers directly behind him as "human wallpaper." Source: Associated Press (AP).

Developing and Constructing Brand Carriers

Developing the main message of a brand is only part of the work of constructing a brand. The brand manager also needs to facilitate the development of brand elements such as names, wordmarks, logos, taglines (slogans), color systems, brand sounds, and visual images, and the development of important carriers of the brand such as products, packages, celebrities, leaders, or the entire organization. The actors involved can choose a more elaborate branding strategy that includes a high number of designed and formalized brand elements, or it can be looser with less fixed elements. A highly designed branding campaign may include a so-called "signature" (a fixed combination of a logotype, a brand mark, and a tagline), selected brand sounds (jingles or signals), fixed typography in texts, and a fully developed and fixed color system. The brand elements including the color system can be used in documents and on letterheads, business cards, websites, vehicles, uniforms, and so forth (see Wheeler 2009 for examples in the private sector). In other cases the branding strategy may involve fewer designed brand elements, for example when the only designed brand elements are a name for the branded product and a supporting tagline.

The meaning of brand elements resides partly in the elements themselves (for example a green logo tends to trigger different emotions than a black logo), but it is also given by stakeholders. It obtains its meaning partly through the performance of the brand as it is perceived by people over time.

The perception of brand elements may be influenced not only through the words used, but also through the visual and the auditory. In some cases, for example place brands or branded products, even smell and tactility may play a role. How does a place smell and what about the noises in a place? How does it feel to touch the product? In short, it is the semiotics in a broad sense that need to be considered and acted upon by the brand manager. In the literature on private brands, a lot of attention has been paid to brand names. Names should be chosen strategically, because they can trigger particular associations. For example the name "Labour" triggers associations with the common people, but names such as "Regeneration action plan" also favor particular associations over others. The brand manager has to decide on this, or facilitate decision processes on this. The same can be said about the semiotics of symbols such as logos and pictorials. Logos may trigger associations with dynamics, progressiveness, or stability, depending on the logo (for an elaborate account of the semiotics of brand elements, see Danesi 2006).

One of the carriers of the brand that may require special attention in governance processes is the organization behind the brand. Brand management may be geared at the behavior of the organization's employees in order to make it fit the brand. The management activities that may be important here are organizing training sessions and involving employees in the development of the organizational strategy and identity. Facilitating behavior that strengthens and communicates the brand is not restricted to organizations, but can also be undertaken in networks of actors.

Altogether, the construction of a brand is not a matter of selecting elements and determining the message in a one-off effort, but rather it is an ongoing process of meaning-making that includes many different activities and may involve stakeholders in many different ways. The meaning of the brand carriers is constantly influenced and changed by communication from stakeholders in the network. Therefore ongoing communication is an integral part of brand management. In the next section, we deal further with the aspect of brand communication.

6.7   BRAND COMMUNICATION: SENDING MESSAGES OR INVOLVING STAKEHOLDERS?

Brand communication is partly a matter of internal communication within an organization or the core of a network (internal branding), and partly external communication to other stakeholders (external branding). A main goal of brand management is to facilitate everybody involved in the organization or network in communicating a coherent message about the brand. The message may be slightly different for different stakeholders, but in essence it should be a coherent message. The brand manager therefore needs to inform everybody and ensure that all contact points with the outside world communicate an appropriate message. This means intensive alignment and informing everybody at touch points, for example street-level bureaucrats and the people who provide services to citizens, but also managers who communicate with particular stakeholders. However, what other actors say about the brand and how they communicate about the brand can never be completely controlled. Particular messages can be facilitated, but communication in a network cannot be controlled. The brand manager may therefore complement his work with forms of relationship management. One cannot control the communications of other actors, but one can work on the relationships with the other actors and thus enhance the chance that they will communicate in favorable ways.

Another strategy is to focus more on building a relationship with consumers through brand communication. In this strategy, the idea is to communicate a particular brand personality to which stakeholders can relate in a relationship between stakeholder and brand that may develop and change over time. An important idea in terms of brand management is that the "brand has to act as a true friend" (Heding et al. 2009, 171). In governance settings however, we think that the relationship between the brand and the person need not necessarily resemble a friendship, but rather approximate a relationship between partners or colleagues. What is important is that there it is a dyadic relationship with some loyalty and trust.

Thirdly and finally, there are communication strategies that are embedded more strongly in the community and culture in which the brand exists. As explained in section 6.4, an important idea in this approach is that the meaning of the brand is created in social interaction among people in a particular community (McAlexander et al. 2002; Muniz and O'Guinn 2001), and that there is exchange between macro level culture and brands (Holt 2004). Because the meaning of the brand is largely determined in a community of people, the brand manager is actually outnumbered. The ability of the brand manager to influence macro cultural processes is limited, and therefore it is important to adjust to these processes, find a good position for the brand in these processes, and try to make the brand profit from them, rather than trying to control them. Actually, this communication strategy comes close to various strategies in network management that emphasize facilitating interaction and trying to reach convergence in perceptions.

Holt (2004) argues that brands may try to become cultural icons by expressing the most general concerns of the time, or at least connecting to them. In this approach, brand management is about adapting to, and using, cultural forces to build a strong brand. Brands evolve in a complex environment. The landscape changes constantly. Brand management becomes a matter of acting in complexity (cf. Teisman et al. 2009), and the best strategy may be to ride the juggernaut (Klijn and Snellen 2009) rather than control the landscape.

Managerial Activities in Brand Communication

Regardless of which one of the three strategies above one chooses, the communication of brands requires a lot of managerial activities in order to arrive at coordinated communication that supports the brand. Managerial activities in brand communication may be directed at: developing a communication plan, determining the content of the message, choosing communication channels, coordinating and facilitating communication activities by stakeholders, enhancing relationships between the brand and its users, and monitoring communications in the environment of the brand.

Developing a communication plan is a crucial activity, because the communication plan forms a guide to the communication of the brand. It specifies the goals of communication and how those goals will be achieved. It clarifies the following elements: communicators, messages, channels, feedback and evaluation, audiences, and time plan. In the communication plan, the brand manager also needs to plan his own role. Does this role concentrate on the communication of the message or does it focus more on the facilitation of communication by others?

The next step is to determine the content of the message (and fit it to the context). Brand values and brand elements are developed as part of the construction of the brand. It must be further specified what exact message one wants to communicate over time. It is important that the content of the message supports the brand values and reproduces the brand elements that one wants to become known among the public, but at the same time the exact content of the message may vary over time and in different contexts.

Choosing communication channels has become an important activity since many channels are available nowadays for communicating a brand. They vary from printed media to broadcast media, including newspapers, leaflets, billboards and other promotion material, websites, social media, television, and radio. When choosing what channels to use, one should take the functional qualities of the channel into account (cf. Leeuwis 2004). Some channels allow for unilateral communication only (e.g. radio), whereas others allow for reciprocal communication (e.g. interactive websites and personal communication). Interactive channels can be used to exchange information in two ways and enhance active learning processes (Leeuwis 2004). Television, newspapers, and popular Internet websites are channels of mass media through which one can reach large audiences, whereas other media such as leaflets reach smaller audiences. Also, as each channel may be favored by different target groups, the channel should be selected in accordance with the target group one wants to reach. If one wishes to reach youngsters, it may be preferable to use social media such as Hyves, Facebook, or Twitter rather than the local newspaper. Another issue is whether the channel allows for receiving the message at a different time than it is produced. Messages diffused via personal communication and radio must be received at the same time as they are produced, and newspapers tend to last only one day. The situation is different if messages are diffused via the Internet and social media. Here, messages can be easily stored and accessed at any time. A final issue is the degree to which one can control the content of the message in a particular channel. Newspapers, for example, select and frame messages in their own way, since they are independent media. One has far more control of the message if one has one's own Internet page.

Coordinating and facilitating stakeholders' communication activities is an important activity since most governance processes involve multiple stakeholders who all communicate with their environment. By coordinating the communication activities around a brand, the brand manager can make the communication activities support and strengthen each other, rather than undermine each other. Communication by others can be facilitated through events where stakeholders or community members meet, or by a particular other context where actors can interact and communicate, for example a website. By actively facilitating the website, one can also exert some control, although too much control is likely to meet resistance and distance the members from the brand. Management of brand communication builds on the idea that communication about the brand spreads fastest and is trusted best if it comes from other members of the community (rather than a marketer or a communication specialist). This means that brand communication is a lot about facilitating communication among members, in particular word of mouth. One way of doing this is to collect and highlight particular stories from community members, which then become more visible and spread more easily within the community. Another management activity is the recruitment and activation of ambassadors of the brand, and facilitation of a network of ambassadors (protagonists of the brand who are willing to promote the brand). Because of the emotional bond that people have with the brand, their enthusiasm for the brand, they may want to contribute to the success of the brand as ambassadors (Heding et al. 2009). If the brand manager aims for the brand to become a cultural icon (Holt 2004), then management activities are geared towards getting the actors to act as cultural activists who stimulate people to think differently. Brand management aims at developing an "authentic populist voice" (Holt 2004, 85).

Brand managers may also deploy activities to enhance communication between the brand and its users through relationships between the brand and its users. Here, the main goal of brand management activities is communication that strengthens the relationship with the users of the brand. In terms of brand communication, the emphasis is on the symbolic value of the brand, and the human characteristics of the brand that add to the brand's personality. There may be less stress on functional qualities of the brand, and more on symbolic and emotional ones. The communication is two way, which means that branding is not only about sending but also very much about receiving messages. Also, communication should not be too pushy since that can easily harm an intimate relationship. An important consideration may be the place and context in which the brand is communicated and present. Like a friend, the brand should be there when needed. For example, for a government or a municipality, it may be crucial to be present when citizens want to be protected or feel safe. Also, if the brand is present in particular contexts, for example particular events or festivals, this may provide the brand a position and meaning in that part of citizens' lives. But apart from being present in particular contexts, public organizations may also manage their brand by creating or facilitating particular contexts. For example, municipalities or political parties may facilitate events or festivals in which the brand of the city or political party can be experienced. The relationship approach stresses management activities that aim to create and facilitate the brand experience, rather than brand promotion or communication. In contrast to more classic approaches—which stress that particular webs of associations can be triggered and stored among target groups—the relationship approach may focus more on providing the context in which a relationship can develop.

But there is more than only providing context. Kotler and Armstrong (2006) use the concept of customer relationship management. An important management activity here is the management of expectations, because it is only if expectations are right that the brand can deliver what is expected. Kotler and Armstrong also stress that organizations may wish to differentiate relationships into basic relationships and full partners, depending on the value of the customer to the company. Of course such differentiation may be unsuitable or even illegitimate for many public organizations when it comes to their relationship with citizens, but, in some governance networks, public organizations could differentiate among stakeholders more easily, depending on how important the stakeholder is to the governance process. Even an organization such as a municipality could offer specific services to its residents that it does not offer to non-residents. The municipality of Barcelona, for example, offers rental bikes to its inhabitants but not to tourists. Also, municipalities may offer reductions to specific groups. For example, elderly people or poor people may receive discounts for the municipal swimming pool or the cultural events in the city.

It is also important to monitor feedback and other communications in the environment. Most communication about a brand is not undertaken or organized by the brand manager; rather, it takes place independent of the brand manager. People talk about brands in their professional and social networks, but the brand may also be discussed on television or in other media far away from the brand managers. Such communications may have a profound influence on how people think about the brand, and so it is crucial to monitor such communications and use them as feedback that may inform the brand owner on what next steps to take in the construction and communication of the brand.

Box 6.3   Wrong Communication or Wrong Brand?

In March 2010, the Ministry of Agriculture, Nature, and Fisheries (LNV) in the Netherlands applies a new way of communicating its policies. It publishes a magazine in the style of the "glossies" that have been very successful in recent years in the Netherlands. Similar to those popular

Continued

glossies, which usually carry the first name of a celebrity, the glossy uses the first name of the minister as its title: *Gerda*.

The popular glossies portray a celebrity and deal with issues relating to the life and career of that celebrity. With the glossy, the ministry attempts to reach new target groups that are not reached by communication in policy documents, newspapers, and serious talk -shows on television. The irony of the medium and the message is not understood however, and certainly not appreciated. The other political parties rally against the initiative and criticize the medium, the style, and the content. The medium is deemed unsuitable because of the high price of producing glossies. Also, the personalized way in which the communication of the ministry's policy has been shaped is criticized. Opponents argue that the glossy is not so much about positioning the ministry and its policies as about providing a vehicle for the minister as a politician of the Christian Democrat Party who wants to publicize and market herself just a few months before the general election. Several parties argue that this would not be a problem so long as the minister used funds from her own political party to do this, and not the budget of the ministry. The debate in parliament becomes rather heated and the campaign is stopped immediately. As a consequence of the glossy, Minister Gerda Verburg faces a difficult time in parliament, where she is accused of, for example, wasting public money. She is forced to apologize, and she has to promise that she will never do this again. This negatively influences her brand as a public manager and political leader.

Figure 6.5   Front page of the glossy magazine *Gerda*.

An Example of Brand Communication

As said earlier classic branding approaches center on the idea that citizens' cognitions and associations can be influenced through sender-oriented communication. Communication in this approach is a matter of getting the word out. As Box 6.3 shows, this can go very wrong if the sender is not sufficiently aware of the context in which the brand is communicated.

The example in Box 6.3 demonstrates that you cannot create just any brand and use any means of communication to promote government policy. Although irony and some exaggeration usually work quite well in the private sector, it is risky for branding government policies. If the style and means of communication are not adapted to the informal rules within the governance network, resistance may be created and have a negative backlash on the brand. The example also shows the importance of actively nurturing and defending a brand at the right time.

6.8 BRAND REPRODUCTION: NOURISHING, SUSTAINING, EVALUATING, AND RENEWING THE BRAND

Brands in ever-changing and contested governance contexts will easily weaken or fade away if nothing is done to reproduce and maintain them. Tellis (2004) makes the point that people's response to a marketing campaign decreases after repeated exposure to it. Therefore branding campaigns need to be rejuvenated regularly. Also, if the governance context changes, it is relevant to adapt the brand accordingly. For example, if there is an increase in public awareness of crime, and citizens increasingly feel unsafe, it may be relevant to focus the political leader's brand more on the issue of crime fighting. However, brands need to be maintained not just because of ongoing changes in the context or rather passively occurring processes of wear, but also because of active criticism and attacks on the brand that occur regularly in governance contexts. This is especially the case if there are conflicting interests and political disputes. If a brand is under attack by political opponents, it will be damaged unless it is well defended. Thus brands have to be updated and must evolve to keep up with the changing political tide, the changing opinions in the governance networks, and changing external conditions.

An important issue in the maintenance and renewal of brands is the degree of continuity and change that is pursued. If brands change too often or too radically, the brand may become blurred and it may confuse or even alienate stakeholders and citizens (cf. Keller 1999). The brand may become less recognized and less trusted. If brands do not change enough, they will wear out or become obsolete. There are different views on continuity and change of brands, with brand managers opting for strategies that differ from slow and partial brand evolution to relatively fast and radical brand revolution. Those who focus on brand identity tend to stress the importance of continuity and slow, gradual evolution. Their argument is that brands revolve around a core identity and that therefore brands cannot change quickly or often, otherwise it becomes unclear whether there is any essence to the brand and what that might be. This argument may apply to organizations that brand themselves with a focus on a core identity. More recently however, several scholars have taken a less essentialist approach to brand identity, arguing that brand identity is constructed in a process of interaction between on the one hand members of the organization, and on the other hand citizens or stakeholders (see e.g. Holt 2002; Csaba and Bengtsson 2006). This leaves more room for dynamics in the brand identity. Keller (1999) argues that the strategic positioning of brands ought to be consistent, whereas tactics such as creative strategies or slogans may be chosen more dynamically. He also argues for brand audits in order to comprehensively examine the health of a brand. On the basis of the brand audit, decisions can be made on retaining or changing the brand position, and on the strategies and tactics that may be applied to sustain or renew the brand.

Strategies for Maintaining and Renewing Brands

Brands can be maintained and renewed through a variety of strategies: brand-oriented strategies (such as brand extension), product-oriented strategies (in governance usually tied to policy content), distribution strategies, competitive strategies, and target group strategies (cf. Keller 1999; Loken et al. 2010).

Brand-oriented strategies aim directly at maintaining or renewing the meaning of the brand, the awareness of the brand, and the brand's breadth. Reinforcing the meaning of a brand is a fruitful strategy of course if a brand evokes strongly positive associations, but if it evokes negative associations or few associations, then renewal of the brand strategy may be the better option. An interesting tactic for renewing the brand meaning may be not to invent some completely new meaning, but to return to the roots of the brand (Keller 1999). For example, a conservative party may return to its origins by focusing on some basic conservative values, while at the same time reducing communication about, for example, government renewal or sustainability. This strategy is rather safe, whereas radical renewal of brand meaning is risky. Returning to the roots usually appeals to existing expectations and images of the past, whereas attempts to change associations radically run the risk of being deliberately ignored by stakeholders or not being remembered by them because the new associations do not fit their expectations. In such cases, evoking new associations may involve an intensive and costly branding campaign. Strategies for increasing awareness of the brand are useful when stakeholders or citizens do not recognize or recall the brand sufficiently. Promotional strategies also come under the heading of awareness strategies. These aim at repetition of the message by advertising it, thus changing the prominence and awareness of the brand. Closely related to raising brand awareness is enlarging a brand's breadth through brand extension. The example of brand extension carried out by Tony Blair, who extended the New Labour brand with the concept of partnerships, has already been discussed in Chapters 1 and 2. Another example of brand extension is the city of The Hague that brands itself as an international city of justice and peace: The Hague launched a campaign together with War Child, thus coupling and reinforcing its own brand with that of the War Child brand.

Apart from strategies aimed at brand meaning, brand managers can also resort to strategies that are product oriented. In a governance context, this refers to strategies that aim to reinforce or renew policy content or services offered. In the case of, for example, city branding, it may also refer to iconic buildings or other physical objects in the city. By adopting a product-oriented strategy, the brand manager tries to work on the brand indirectly, by working on the product.

The idea behind this strategy is that the experience and image of the brand is also largely determined by the experience of the branded object. This strategy is especially valuable if the quality of the services or the results of a policy in reality lag far behind what is communicated via the brand. Failure to address such a reality gap can be disastrous for the brand. Another form of product-oriented strategy is the introduction of new products, for example new policies or services, in order to broaden the relevance of the brand and reach new target groups. Although introducing new policies and services is an important aspect of product-oriented strategies, it should not be forgotten that ending particular policies and services is equally important, especially if they have become irrelevant or unpopular.

Distribution strategies aim to maintain or renew the brand by communicating the brand through new channels or by involving new stakeholders who spread the word about the brand. As explained in section 6.7 on communicating brands, the usage of new channels may help to reach new audiences and to increase the exposure of the brand. For further reading on issues of distribution and communication, see section 6.7.

Competitive strategies for maintaining and renewing a brand refer to strategies to extend a brand into an area that has been dominated by another brand—for example if one department starts to brand itself as an actor in a specific policy field that has so far been dominated by another department. But brands can also be strategically positioned in relation to the competition, for example if a new political party finds a lacuna in the political landscape and develops a brand that specifically aims to fill that gap. This strategy is also partly about reaching new audiences and target groups. An important task in maintaining brands is to make sure that new stakeholders or developing societal groups are sufficiently reached by the brand. Policy brands and political brands also should appeal to new cohorts of people; political parties for example must appeal to young voters, but governmental organizations also face the challenge of reaching young people if they want to attract young talent into their workforce. This may require rejuvenating the brand and adapting it to the life world of new groups. More generally, it is important for brand managers to regularly identify what groups are reached and what groups are largely missed.

As a final remark on the maintenance and renewal of brands, it should be noted that it can also be decided to retire a brand when the environment has changed so much that the brand is simply "not worth saving" (Keller 1999, 119). This is common practice in governance landscapes; brands of policies or leaders are regularly abandoned when the policy itself is terminated, or when the leader becomes unpopular. It must be noted, however, that it is equally common for the policy itself not to be changed very much but rather continue to exist under another name or brand. Another form of retiring brands is found in cases where political leaders are replaced by new leaders.

Defending the Brand: Protecting against Counter Branding and Eroding

Governance processes are often characterized by conflicting interests and struggle among stakeholders. Brands may also become subjected to such struggle, and then they are likely to become damaged. Actors may use counter-branding strategies, in which they creatively alter existing brands and try to give them new meaning (see also the example of counter branding the George W. Bush brand in section 2.6). If governance processes become politicized, defending brands becomes especially important. However, it is not only in situations of political struggle that brand defense is important, because it also deserves attention in brand communities, particularly in the form of damage limitation. Firstly, particular groups in brand communities can "hijack" the brand and give their particular meaning to it. Here, an active form of meaning-making by the brand manager is important. In brand communities, the aspect of rumor control is important—for example, in the Apple community rumors about new versions of the i-Phone spread quickly and they may damage sales of existing i-Phones. Similarly, rumors about a leader's retirement from politics may damage his or her position, as the actors around the leader may quickly start to orient themselves more to possible successors. In many (small) municipalities rumors can spread quickly and come to play a damaging role if there is not a strategy of rumor control. Brands with a high profile, so-called cultural icons, are likely to be subjected to counter-branding activities by multiple stakeholders. In the private sector, McDonald's has suffered from counter-branding activities, probably because it has become such a well-known symbol of industrialized and unhealthy food production, as well as American culture. In the public sector, politicians or movements that become a strong brand or even a cultural icon are commonly attacked, for example the Tea Party movement in the US, which has been under fierce attack.

Several strategies can be used to defend a brand. First of all, there is the pro-active strategy of involving all stakeholders and users of the brand in the production of the brand. Giving them a say in the meaning of the brand decreases the chance of their attacking the brand later on. Secondly, pro-active and reactive strategies of rumor control can be deployed. Pro-active rumor control refers to an active communication of the brand values and brand meaning by the brand owner. We have already discussed communication strategies in section 6.7, but we wish to reiterate here the importance of developing good relationships with multiple stakeholders. One cannot control exactly what people communicate about a brand, but if one builds good relationships with actors they will not communicate negatively about the brand, and therefore relationship management is an important aspect of damage control. Reactive strategies of defending brands refer to providing counter arguments against criticism, but it is probably even more important to provide counter images against images that damage the brand. A final strategy is to ignore criticism, but this is viable only if the source of the critique has little communication power.

6.9 CONCLUSION AND REFLECTION: BRANDING AS AN ONGOING PROCESS

This chapter has argued that brands in governance processes need to be managed if they are to have an impact and remain relevant in a constantly changing governance environment. The dynamics in governance processes require a continuous form of brand management, rather than a one-shot branding campaign. Brand management in a governance process is an ongoing process, carried out not only by a single brand owner but by multiple stakeholders.

The management of brands can be seen as a relatively new strategy for managing governance processes. As a management approach in governance processes, brand management can be used alongside other management approaches such as network management. Network management is oriented primarily towards the management of interactions and network structures, whereas brand management is primarily oriented towards managing perceptions. As we have seen in this chapter however, they often support each other or are fairly close to one another.

This chapter has dealt with several main components of brand management, such as market research, brand construction, brand communication, and brand maintenance. The challenge for brand managers is to develop a form of brand management in which the different components are well aligned. It is counterproductive to organize a massive brand communication campaign if the branded policy is malfunctioning or impossible to implement.

In this chapter we have discussed what brand managers can do about brand development. We laid out the strategies and tactics they can use, and the activities in which they can engage. Thus, the stress was on the opportunities to manage brands; but of course the manageability of brands in complex governance environments is limited, and brand managers face numerous difficulties and challenges when they deploy branding strategies. The next chapter deals more extensively with the risks and limits of branding.

7 Risks and Limits of Branding

7.1 INTRODUCTION

The Case of Branding the Øresund Region

The Øresund area surrounds the Strait of Øresund that lies between Denmark and Sweden, and encompasses the cities of Copenhagen and Malmö. The Øresund area has been branded as one region in order to connect the Danish and the Swedish communities, and present the region in a more coherent way to investors and tourists (see also Chapters 2 and 4). The idea is to reconstruct the existing image of the region as a peripheral area, and brand it as a modern, competitive region and a creative hub (Hospers 2006). An important player in the development and branding of the region is the Øresund committee, which provides a platform for political representatives from regional and local authorities in the region (Hospers 2006; Stenberg 1998). The committee carries out projects, thereby often partnering with several public and private parties. The committee has also been involved in policy development, mainly on public transportation, environmental policies, and the labor market (Stenberg 1998). According to several commentators, the development of the Øresund region can be considered a success; the region has done positively in economic terms (especially production and employment rates), and a defensive and non-cooperative attitude between the parties on both sides of the Danish–Swedish border has diminished (see e.g. Hospers 2006; OECD 2003). However, the extent to which the branding campaign has been a success is debatable. Stenberg, a project coordinator of the Øresund committee, argues that there is a commitment among regional opinion makers to raise public awareness about the region's strong points and the benefits of regional cooperation (Stenberg 1998). There have been several efforts to involve stakeholders in the creation of the brand; for example, a workshop was held in London in which a group of participants arrived at consensus about making the concept of "The Human Capital" central to the Øresund brand (Pedersen 2004). However, despite all good intentions, the broader public has never really engaged in the branding of Øresund. Participation in the branding process mainly involved a selected group of stakeholders in focus groups. Many voices of the people were excluded during the development of the campaign, because the main stakeholders had the inclination to accommodate the global market rather than the public within the region (Pedersen 2004). Although the branding campaign was also partly targeted at the inhabitants of the region, the people in the area do not feel part of the Øresund community, and they do not feel an Øresund identity (Hamers 2005). The Øresund region is something projected and imagined by a political and business elite, rather than a broadly shared identity (Hamers 2005; Hospers 2006). Further, cooperation between the countries may have increased significantly, but several cross-border issues have continued. Notwithstanding the wish to brand the region as a unity, there has been an ongoing discussion about where the Øresund committee should be physically located. Cross-border cooperation sometimes remains difficult, as tellingly illustrated by Hamers (2005) who mentions a difficulty for the bureaucracy: there is a different distance between the holes made in sheets of paper by the perforators on each side of the border.

Risks and Limits of Branding

The example of the Øresund region highlights two main issues. Firstly, it is not easy to use branding successfully in governance processes. The case shows that there are risks to branding in the sense that branding processes can take forms that ignore local citizens and that are biased towards specific other target groups (in this case international companies operating in the global market). Lack of attention to local citizens' ideas illustrates a problematic relationship between branding and democratic governance that may occur during branding processes. In this case, the content of the brand did not reflect the identity of the region as experienced by most people. The brand reflects an identity to which a limited group of stakeholders aspire, rather than a broadly shared idea about the region. The support for the brand among the companies and the private sector in the region is probably significant, but this is not the case among the citizens and the communities in the area. There is a gap between the reality as perceived by the citizens in the region, and the image projected by the brand. One could argue that the brand in a sense obscures certain problems in the region, namely, that it is not a region united by a shared feeling of identity. The branding process in Øresund shows that branding in the public sector may raise ethical and normative questions, which often have to do with the functioning of democracy.

Secondly, the Øresund case exemplifies the possible limitations to the effects of branding. The branding campaign has not altered the perceptions of the inhabitants about their region, although the campaign may have been successful in influencing perceptions of investors outside the region. In terms of the effects of the brand, it is uncertain what exactly the branding campaign has contributed to improvements in cross-border cooperation and governance of the region. As we explain in this chapter, the effectiveness of branding can be questioned, especially in relation to effects beyond the realm of symbolic representation, that is, effects in terms of the development and implementation of governance processes.

Not surprisingly, there is debate in the literature about the limitations and risks of branding (see e.g. Blichfeldt 2005; Greenberg 2008; Holt 2002; Klein 2000; Kotler and Kotler 1999; O'Shaugnessy 2001; Stigel and Frimann 2006). Branding has been criticized for leading to sketching overly rosy pictures, furthering a selective provision of information to citizens, or even worse, the outright misleading of people. To this criticism it can be added that branding uses people's unconscious to trigger associations and ideas without people being aware of it (e.g. Batey 2008). In this sense, branding runs the risk of manipulation. Branding may readily be framed as propaganda when it is perceived to be manipulative. Interestingly, such criticism of branding implicitly assumes that branding works effectively. It presumes that marketers and their brands shape people's ideas to a high degree. In this model, brand managers are cultural engineers who effectively influence how people feel and think (cf. Holt 2002), but of course this assumption can also be criticized for underestimating people's agency and overestimating the authority of brand managers.

In this chapter, we trawl through the literature and discuss both the risks and the limitations of branding. In section 7.2, we discuss the risks of branding in relation to ethical considerations and issues of democracy. In section 7.3, we elaborate on limitations in the effects of branding; this is related to issues of manageability and the working of brands in governance processes. In the final section of this chapter, 7.4, we draw conclusions and discuss the responses that marketing scholars and practitioners have given with regard to the critical remarks on the risks and limitations of branding.

7.2 RISKS OF BRANDING: ISSUES REGARDING ETHICS AND DEMOCRACY

The literature mentions a number of risks associated with branding. Some of these risks apply to all forms of branding; some of them relate more exclusively to branding in governance processes. In general, we can distinguish four major risks that have been identified:

1. A focus on marketing, sales, and consumption (of public services) runs contrary to the resolution of collective problems as this requires deliberation and active citizenship (e.g. Walsh 1994).
2. There is the potential for biased communication and manipulation of the public (e.g. Greenberg 2008; Paddison 1993).

3. Branding and marketing enhance a populist agenda and discourage addressing unpopular issues (see e.g. Reeves et al. 2006; Walsh 1994 for discussions on this subject).
4. Branding may neglect the public during both brand development and the implementation of branding campaigns (e.g. Flowerdew 2004; Kavaratzis 2008).

The first two risks are the most prominent in the literature, and so we give them the most attention in this section.

Tensions between Branding, Democracy, and Public Sector Goals

The concept of branding comes from the private sector. With the upsurge of branding in the public sector, the application of the private sector strategy in a public sector context has also been criticized (e.g. Greenberg 2008; Walsh 1994). Critics argue that the main goal in the private sector is to maximize profits by delivering and selling goods and services. The public sector, however, has more and broader aims. Governments govern by taking political decisions, and developing policies and regulations. Whereas the private sector focuses on efficiency, political decision making is not only about efficiency but also about moral issues and what is good for the community. This means that the relation between citizens and the state can be characterized as fulfilling two roles at the same time: the citizen as consumer (of public services such as education, social services, safety, and so forth), and the citizen as active democratic participant. Public sector governance always has to deal with both roles at the same time. As we have argued before, governance processes are also about dealing with conflicting values (see Chapters 1, 3, and 6). This requires some form of democratic deliberation based on active citizenship and collective commitment rather than consuming government services (Walsh 1994). Political dialogue between governments and citizens is crucial here, and this cannot be replaced by a marketing approach of public branding (Walsh 1994). Thus although brands can motivate and communicate, they are not a replacement for the deliberation process between actors with conflicting values.

Actually, brands that focus on images, emotions, and heuristics may even hinder dialogue and decision making. There are two main reasons why brands that evoke strong emotions and images may exclude reflection and discussion about values and alternatives. The first reason is that the emotions and images may be so strong and dominant that they can hardly be challenged and changed through deliberation. The second reason is that the emotions and images invoked by brands are partly unconscious, and thus not amenable to deliberation. More deliberate forms of democracy, like most governance processes that are built on the idea that preferences are changed by deliberation, discussion, and reasonable argumentation (see Dryzek 2000; Held 2006), would thus suffer from brands centering on strong emotions and images. The more brands with their accompanying images and emotions are (unconsciously) vested in citizens' minds, the more difficult it is to perform these kinds of deliberative processes.

Brands as Distorted Representation of Reality

Branding is also criticized for not always giving a truthful representation of reality, being potentially manipulative and detrimental to truthful communication to citizens. It has been said that branding in the public sector may appear as a form of spinning that prevents the public from acquiring a proper understanding of what their government is doing (e.g. Brownill 1994; Holcomb 1994; Greenberg 2008). Somewhere, there is a thin line between creating brands and overstepping the line into propaganda, which has a very negative association since authoritarian regimes have often made successful use of propaganda to deceive the public. Thus even a hint of propaganda readily rebounds against branding, as the communication example of the Dutch ministry of agriculture in Chapter 6 also shows.

Several authors have addressed this problem in the literature on place branding, arguing that place branding focuses on positive aspects of cities and easily conceals certain harsh realities of urban life. Paddison (1993) for example has argued that Glasgow's marketing campaign tended to overlook social deprivation and poverty in the city. Greenberg (2008) argues that the New York City branding campaign has one-sidedly constructed an image of New York as an attractive tourist destination and the main financial center in the world. The branding campaign was dominated by efforts to enhance the economic position of the city, at the expense of articulating working-class identities or such underground movements of youth culture as hip-hop and punk (Greenberg 2008). As Waitt argues in his research on Sydney, images used to market the city of Sydney for the Olympic games in 2000 involved a "redefinition of social 'realities' through the prism of the Olympic ideology" (Waitt 1999, 1074). Waitt shows how the ethnic diversity in Sydney is presented in terms of a rich cultural community, employed to celebrate differences and the "cohesive unity within that diversity" (Waitt, 1999, 1065). This image accommodates the Olympic ideal of international goodwill and friendship between diverse people. Waitt, however, argues that such a portrayal of Sydney ignores ongoing socio-spatial polarization and ethnic concentrations.

The examples of Glasgow, New York, and Sydney clarify a risk inherent in branding, and that is that reality becomes selectively redefined in order to please a certain target group, for example the Olympic committee in the case of Sydney, or tourists and large international companies in the case of New York. Also, branding tends to have a bias towards positive representations due to the very "the nature of the marketing project" (Paddison 1993, 343). Actually, this risk is related to the first risk that was discussed. If brands also infer choices about the images they present, and thus which values are emphasized, they can inhibit a freer and deliberate process where citizens discuss these values.

This kind of criticism can also be found in some of the literature on political marketing and political branding. In creating brands for political leaders and political events, branding regularly "edits the truth," as for instance in political commercials that mention debates and news conferences that never took place, or that stereotype opponents (O'Shaughnessy 2001).[1] Another form of editing the truth is "spinning," which refers to "affixing a desirable interpretation on to a still mobile situation" (O'Shaughnessy 2001, 1051). For example, the Labour government of Tony Blair in the UK, but also the George W. Bush government in the US, were connected with spinning (Bennett 2009; Fairclough 2000; O'Shaughnessy 2001).

Thus this critique of branding posits that there is a thin line between branding, spinning, and propaganda. Examination of the critical literature suggests that the greatest risk of branding is not that it can be used to communicate outright lies or gross exaggeration (this would be discovered by the public soon enough) but rather that it involves forms of spinning, i.e. giving information a certain twist (spin) to construct a message in a specific (biased) way.

The critique that brands can become manipulative is fueled by the argument that branding is partly based on influencing the unconscious. If governments or governance networks influence what people think without people knowing it, this may pose a risk to several democratic values. It may hamper free deliberation of the people, because one cannot deliberate freely (free of coercion or manipulation) if one is being manipulated without knowing it. Besides, the democratic value of the consent of the governed is compromised when individuals are influenced unconsciously, and finally transparency is under threat.

In summary, branding has been criticized for its tendency to emphasize those aspects that are attractive to the target groups and to emphasize positive aspects over negative ones. An economic rationale may come to dominate branding practices, thus possibly conflicting with other rationales linked to the identities and life worlds of various social groups and communities. Critical scholars have pointed to the possibility of branding becoming manipulative.

Of course this critique has also reached marketing scholars and practitioners (e.g. Kavaratzis 2008; Lees-Marshment 2004; Reeves et al. 2006). Some of their responses are that manipulative and untruthful marketing cannot work for long. If people come to realize that a brand does not deliver what it promises (and marketers argue that people will come to realize it after some time), their trust in the brand will diminish and the popularity and the power of the brand will decrease (Lees-Marshment 2004). Marketers have argued that marketing and branding are not about creating an unrealistic or overly positive picture, but rather about finding out how people perceive something, especially what they like about it, and then use that to create the image of the brand (e.g. Kotler and Armstrong 2006).

Branding as a Populist Agenda or as Ignoring the Public

Branding as a marketing approach starts from consumer wishes and making the product that consumers want. Critics have argued that the drawback of applying such an approach in a governance context is that it leads to a focus on popular issues, and taking only decisions that are popular among the people. It may lead to the neglect of less popular or less well-known issues, and to avoiding decisions that are unpopular but necessary.[2] This is a warning not to follow uncritically the wishes that citizens articulate. This critique points at the risk of overemphasizing the importance of citizens' wants and needs and neglecting the importance of putting those wants and needs into the perspective of all governmental responsibilities. But this can also be extended to the process in governance. As we have seen in this book, governance processes are about solving complex value conflicts and searching for new innovative solutions to solve those value conflicts. For innovation, reflection is needed, as is looking beyond existing solutions and knowledge. One can imagine that brands, certainly if strongly anchored in the actor's perceptions, could block innovative solutions. In this way, brands' populist character could inhibit the flexibility and innovation needed in most governance processes.

Whereas some authors have highlighted the risk of listening too much to the needs and wishes of the people, others have argued that branding ignores the people. Several scholars have conducted research in which they found that branding was organized by elites of public and private managers who take strategic decisions, thereby bypassing elected politicians (Bennett and Savani 2003) and the citizenry (Kavaratzis 2008). Branding then becomes a tool in the hands of the elite that ignores the wishes and identities of ordinary people. Consequently, branding becomes a risk to democratic legitimacy. In a similar vein, Greenberg (2008), but also authors such as Broudehoux (2001), have argued that private parties have such a big say in branding campaigns that this has become a form of policymaking by (economic) elites and private parties that escapes the democratic control mechanisms.

Thus, to conclude, the literature on branding discusses a number of risks involved in using branding in general or in governance processes specifically. In particular, the public character of governance processes makes branding slightly more tricky than when it is used in the private sphere. Branding may be a risk to democratic decision making if it is applied in ways that breach implicit and explicit democratic rules.

7.3   LIMITS OF BRANDING: ISSUES AROUND THE EFFECTIVENESS OF BRANDING

In the preceding chapters, we have laid stress on the working of brands, often putting emphasis on what brands can do. But of course brands are not magical instruments to solve all problems of communication and joint action in the media society; there is a long list of limitations to what branding can achieve. Some of those limitations have already been touched upon in sections 2.6 and 3.4, but so far they have not been elaborated upon. In this section, we discuss limitations in the effectiveness of branding by distinguishing three main sources of limitations:

1. The first category of limitation is rooted in the idea that brands are coupled to reality. Brands need to correspond with reality to a certain degree, and this poses certain limits to the messages that can be communicated through brands.
2. The second category of limitation relates to the stakeholders or target groups of the branding process. Questions can be raised as to whether brands (symbols) can influence their perceptions effectively, even more so if they are meant to influence perceptions of widely varying groups with various preoccupations and interests.
3. The third category of limitation pertains to limits in influencing action and decision making in governance processes. For example, to what extent does the influence of brands reach beyond the cognitive and actually alter decision making in governance processes?

Correspondence to Reality Poses Limitations to Branding

In a way, brands are strange entities. On the one hand, brands are created images that evoke associations and emotions that may go beyond what relates directly to the branded services, policies, or policy products in governance processes. On the other hand, brands are confined and limited by what is going on in reality, because brands need to deliver on the brand promise, or otherwise they will lose credibility and popularity (Kotler et al. 1999; Loken et al. 2010). In governance processes, this implies that the expectations raised by a brand must be backed up by performance in terms of policy development and implementation. This can include services delivered, policy initiatives to be implemented, or changes made to service delivery and policy proposals. In other words, brands become meaningful and trustworthy if they are aligned with concrete developments in the governance process (see also Eshuis and Edelenbos 2009). Thus, if a policy in a certain area is branded as tough on crime and the result is branded as a promising new beginning, it is difficult to brand it successfully if the newspapers are full of new crimes every day in the area and crime figures are rising.

In place branding, this implies that the city brand is confined in the sense that it needs to reflect social, economic, and physical developments in the city or the region. The communication about a place through logos, slogans, and images should be consistent with the primary messages coming from the physical streetscape and the people in the area (Eshuis and Edelenbos 2009). In terms of the limitations of branding, this means that the message that a brand can credibly communicate is limited by the developments in the governance process.

However, the brand is limited not only by the reality of the product, service, or policy, but also by the original image and its associations with citizens and other stakeholders. It is, therefore, extremely difficult to create a tough policy image on crime in certain neighborhoods when the original image is that of a crime-infested neighborhood. Even if crime figures go down, the broad image of a crime-infested neighborhood is likely to persist over a prolonged period. Media and spectators may for instance continue to see and report the still-existing crime and magnify that instead of focusing on the reduction. For this reason, it is very hard to create new brands for neighborhoods that have a bad image. It requires long and hard work on the side both of the branding process and of the delivery, and that process is easily thwarted by incidents, negative media attention, a prominent figure voicing skepticism, and so on. The complexity and unpredictability of governance processes further enhance the possibility that the branding process will stagnate somewhere.

Thus, brands and branding also show path dependency; they are influenced and partly shaped by past history. They are not easily changed because images in people's minds are not changed overnight. People may see the world not through the prism of the newly created brand but rather through the prism of the existing images. This means that often—for example in the case of places, policies, and political parties that have a strong profile among stakeholders—objects cannot be successfully branded at will. They remain complex packages of goods with a specific history.

Actors' Autonomy and Interpretive Processes Pose Limits to Influencing Their Perceptions

A lot of the literature on branding seems to start from the assumption that actors' perceptions are easily influenced by marketing and branding. Now, the fast rise of marketing, advertising, and brand value seems to confirm this, but actually we do not yet fully know the effects of brands. Not surprisingly, a main line of criticism is that brands have only limited effects on actors' perceptions, and, if they have effects, these cannot be entirely controlled or managed. The usual explanation for this is roughly that brands are symbols that acquire meaning through interpretive processes, and this means that actors may imbue brands with different meanings than originally meant by brand managers. The meaning that brand managers "encode" in the brand may not be the same as the meaning that citizens "decode" (O'Shaughnessy 2001). This is especially the case in governance processes with multiple actors, both public and (semi) private, who interpret brands from a particular disposition, which is determined by their own background and interests.

The capacity of brands to influence perceptions may be further limited because the *genre* of marketing messages negatively influences their credibility (Koller 2009). According to Koller, audiences can be expected to be aware or even cynical of the motives behind marketing and promotion, which makes "uncritical acceptance of the communicated brand image unlikely" (Koller 2009, 20). This idea is affirmed by Holt's (2002) analysis of consumers' resistance practices. They deliberately try to filter out marketing manipulation. The resistance of actors against brands may even take the shape of active counter branding. As explained already in Chapter 2, brands in the public sector are often contested if the values that are inherent in the brands are contested. Given the fact that governance processes often include conflicting and contested values, counter branding is likely to occur. Counter branding may prove a difficulty for those who initiated the original brand, but from a perspective of plurality counter branding can be seen more positively because it enhances the expression of different of opinions; this is important to the democratic deliberative processes.

In governance processes, it is not only actors themselves that can give brands a meaning that may not be intended by the brand developers; the media also may ascribe unplanned interpretations to brands. As argued in Chapter 5, media attention can be uncontrollable. It can change the construction of policy problems and the meaning of brands. This may in turn influence the interpretations that stakeholders develop of the brand.

Consequently, the meaning of brands cannot be entirely controlled; one can control the associations that are constructed around the brand. Brands do provide a way to convey meaning to multiple stakeholders, but it should be recognized that "brand meanings proliferate in unexpected ways" (Hatch and Rubin 2006, 41). Hatch and Rubin further argue that in the long term also the meaning of brands may change in unpredictable ways. They state that "a brand's contemporary significance results from collective interpretations by multiple stakeholders over numerous but particular historical moments" (Hatch and Rubin 2006, 41). They make the point that the interpretation of brands is not only an individual process, but also part of collective interpretive processes. This also seems valuable in the context of governance processes that are followed by the media and the public.[3] Thus through media attention and joint invocations of the meaning of the brand by multiple actors, certain interpretations of brands may be enforced upon the brand whereby the brand receives a quite different meaning than intended by the initiator.

The Øresund example has already raised the question as to what effects a branding campaign has on people's perceptions. The case gives credence to the proposition that it is the daily reality that determines how people think about their place, not the place brand. It may be argued that visitors less familiar with the daily life in a place may be more susceptible to the images evoked by the brand.

In other words, and this brings us to the next main limitation of brands posited in the literature, people's perceptions are influenced probably just as strongly by factors other than brands (O'Shaughnessy 2001). According to O'Shaughnessy (2001), the effects of political marketing are often transcended by factors such as press activism. He gives the example of the British Labour Party in 1992 under Neil Kinnock, who were running an election campaign involving serious marketing and branding efforts. They were leading in the polls until the British press, in particular the newspaper *The Sun*, decided to turn against Labour. They demonized Labour, for example through an "eight page pre-election special 'Nightmare on Kinnock Street'" (O'Shaughnessy 2001, 1055). It is therefore not surprising that Blair, before he started his successful election campaign of 1997, made peace with the tabloids and with Rupert Murdoch, the owner of *The Sun*. This helped Blair to achieve what Labour leaders before him could not: receive a favorable assessment from the tabloids. The impact of political marketing should therefore "be seen in the context of often more significant drivers of political influence" (O'Shaughnessy 2001, 1055). One could also argue that the Neil Kinnock case does not show the ineffectiveness of branding, but rather the importance of counter branding (by the media), and the impossibility for a brand owner to control the meaning of the brand. As already stated, where there is a high number of stakeholders with diverging interests, brands may develop in unexpected ways.

The existence of a multiplicity of stakeholders in governance processes limits the possibilities of branding anyhow, apart from the fact that they have different interpretations of the brand. Even though brands try to appeal to different groups and evoke different associations with them, this has its limits. A brand that is suitable for one group (e.g. tourists) may not suit other groups (e.g. residents) (Bennett and Savani 2003). This may be even more relevant for governance processes than for private settings. In a commercial context, firms can choose target groups and ignore other groups, but in a public context it may be inappropriate or impossible to ignore groups of residents, voters, or businesses. It often proves difficult to create a brand that fits the preferences of all interest groups. Stigel and Frimann (2006) encountered this limitation of branding in their study of the branding of two Danish towns, on the basis of which they concluded that the wish or need to arrive at consensus about brand identities easily leads to brands with only very general and nondescript values. This inhibits the effectiveness of the brand in terms of creating a distinguishable identity and making the place stand out among its competitors.

In governance processes where actors have to deal with an overload of information, it may be difficult to create brand awareness. Thus, even if one assumes that brands can effectively influence perceptions, one would need to take into account whether the brand actually reaches its target groups. In modern governance processes, one can potentially reach many people through mass media and social media, so this is not the problem. The difficulty, however, is to stand out and attract attention in the context of all the messages and competing brands out there. There are limits to the attention people pay to a brand in a context of information overload, even if brands are rather effective in drawing on the visual and emotional to attract attention.

Limited Effects of Branding in Governance Processes

Even if one discarded the previous criticism and accepted that brands influence perceptions of actors in governance processes, the question still remains as to what the relation is between perception and action. It is well known that perceptions and motivations do not always lead to related actions. People have favorable attitudes towards sustainable development, but these very often do not result in actions that are in line with this commitment. In governance processes, this relation between perceptions and agency is even more problematic. Governance processes require the joint collective action of various actors in the governance networks. Thus it is not only one actor that has to relate its actions to perceived problems; more actors also have to engage in this. The fact that brands need to effectively influence the actions of various actors at the same time makes the problem of branding effectiveness considerably more difficult.

The question is thus not only the extent to which brands can influence actions of individuals, but also the extent to which they can enhance action that is coordinated and sustained over a longer period. In order to realize this, brands must have more effects than just triggering particular associations. Branding campaigns need not only to trigger particular associations time and again, but also to convince people and intrinsically motivate them. The question then is what are the effects of branding, beyond the symbolic? To what extent do brands change concrete decisions and implementation of policies? The effectiveness of branding on these points has not yet been empirically proven.

As for the regulatory power of brands, Blichfeldt's (2005) work addresses the limited power of internal branding (i.e. the influencing of the behavior of employees within a branded organization or residents within a branded place. Blichfeldt (2005, 396–97) argues that "locals are beyond marketers' direct control (unless the resident in question is working for the marketer)." Therefore she argues that there is no reason why residents would act "in ways that strengthen 'marketer-chosen' brand associations" (Blichfeldt 2005, 397). This point is relevant to governance processes, especially in cases where there are multiple stakeholders with a degree of autonomy to decide on their own actions. Even if stakeholders agree on a particular brand, for example a brand that puts the concept of sustainability center stage, they will not allow the brand or the brand manager to dictate that their behavior should always be in line with the sustainability brand.

But the connection between frame and action, and the difficulty of many actors having to act collectively, is not the only problem that one faces when looking at the effects of brand. Just as brands can be counter branded, the situation may also arise that they have to compete with other brands; and, if they have to compete with other brands, their effects on the behavior of actors may be limited too. Competing brands may draw attention away from each other's audiences, thus diminishing the effects of each brand on the audience. Or competing brands may even run counter to each other's images, thus undermining each other's images and decreasing each other's effectiveness. This is for example the case in political arenas where brands of different political parties often undermine each other. Thus, it can be argued that branding merely creates competition at a symbolic level, but that it would not improve the public sector as a whole if everybody started to brand themselves. The cities that brand themselves are only increasing their mutual competition, but if every city spends 1,000,000 Euro a year on branding, in the end nobody profits. It only costs money. Those in particular who doubt the effectiveness of branding may come to argue that branding draws away scarce resources (in order to create symbols) at the expense of primary processes in the public sector, such as guaranteeing public safety or restructuring communities.

The high costs of branding campaigns are not only relevant in terms of how public money is spent, but may also create problems in terms of branding. If people come to see the use of public money for a branding campaign as a waste of money, this may negatively influence the brand itself because it then becomes associated with misuse, extravagance, and ruinous capitalism.

7.4   CONCLUSION AND DISCUSSION

Brands have their limitations; that is certain after the discussion in this chapter. We have made a distinction between risks (pertaining to ethical and normative problems) and limitations (related to effectiveness) of branding. The most important limitations have to do with the fact that there is still no certainty about the effects of brands on perceptions. It is not fully clear whether and how brands have an impact on people's cognitions. And subsequently, if brands do influence perceptions, it is indeterminate whether this results in concrete changes in behavior. Other limitations of branding relate to features of the public sector, in particular the complexity and limited manageability of governance processes. The fact that actors have differing and even opposing perceptions often causes conflict that may result in different non-linear and complex dynamics (see e.g. Gerrits 2008; Teisman et al. 2009). There may be all kinds of dynamics that steer away perceptions from the meaning that brand managers try to establish. Thus it may well be, and we have given some arguments for it in this chapter, that the effects of brands are even more problematic in governance processes than in a private setting.

The risks of branding relate to ethical problems, rather than to the question of whether brands influence actors' perceptions. They relate to the question of how far we can go in influencing perceptions at all, especially in the case of creating associations that work their way into the mind by more indirect and unconscious processes. And of course the question of whether brands hinder or block democratic deliberative processes is an important one.

Difficulties with Branding: A Pragmatic Position

So far, on the basis of empirical research, it has not been easy to decipher the puzzle of whether branding is effective or not. Although large amounts of money are spent on brands and branding, and although there are indications that brands can be highly effective as various political campaigns such as those of Blair and Obama seem to indicate, definite evidence is hard to get. Thus the situation remains that some argue that branding is a highly effective tool, whereas critics point at its limitations. Some argue that branding poses risks to democracy because it does not inform—but rather manipulates—the public. However, others argue that brands are perfect tools for communication in a visual culture where people have neither the time nor the interest to absorb detailed policy programs.

In our view, both positions have credibility, and the issue of effectiveness is also an empirical one. Future research will have to prove the value and effectiveness of brands in different contexts. This will not always be an easy task, since proving relations between changes in perceptions and actual behavior remains difficult. In the meanwhile, public managers, politically elected officials, and appointees find themselves in situations where they need new ways to communicate with a wide group of stakeholders and motivate them. Branding has become a reality in public administrative life in general, and governance processes in particular, and this alone demands research activities in this field. If negative effects of brands in governance processes are observed, those should be documented and explained. Consequently, the perspective in this book is a rather pragmatic one: branding is a growing phenomenon in governance because more and more public managers consider it useful to them. It is, therefore, a phenomenon that must be well understood and critically examined.

Taking the Ethical Issues Seriously

Interestingly, there is a relation between the ethical issues and the perception that scholars and practitioners may have of the effectiveness of branding. If one thinks that branding is a highly effective tool, then this also implies that it is a potentially dangerous tool. If one believes that branding is highly effective for managing perceptions, then this could be a risk in an ethical sense if it misused. This is the position taken by critics of branding and neoliberalist capitalism such as Naomi Klein (2000) and Mary Douglas Vavrus (2007): they see branding as an extremely manipulative tool, thus implicitly acknowledging its effectiveness in terms of managing perceptions.

If one is critical about the effects of branding, then this seems to imply that the ethical risks of, for example, manipulation are also less. In short, we feel that it is important to discuss the limits and risks of branding, because either branding is a highly effective strategy with ethical risks, or there is a problem with the effectiveness of branding and that should be taken into account. At the same time, one would be on slippery ground if one argued that branding is both a risk to democracy and a sloppy strategy in terms of effectiveness.

All in all, a lot of work has yet to be done, both in terms of understanding empirically how branding is employed in governance processes and what its effects are, and in terms of the normative and ethical problems that occur when branding is applied in a democratic governance context. These ethical issues have to be taken seriously, even more so in cases where branding effectively influences people's perceptions actions.

8 Brands and Governance
Towards Interactive Forms of Branding

8.1 INTRODUCTION

In this book, we have gone into the rise of branding and the use of branding in governance processes. Branding is now everywhere in our daily life as we observed. The large majority of private products are sold and marketed with the aid of branding, and established brands have a huge economic value (Kotler et al. 1999). We have argued that, although the expansion of brands and branding in governance is far less than in the private sector, there is significant growth here. In the political sphere, marketing has increased rapidly, and especially in western countries most political campaigns use branding activities to promote political leaders and political programs. There has also been a significant increase in place branding all over the world; and we are seeing the first attempts to use branding as a strategy for managing perceptions in complex governance processes.

This is not surprising because, as argued in this book, branding fits the shift towards a mediatized society where visual images and information overload have become predominant in everyday life as well as in governance processes. Brands fit in this trend towards the visual and towards communicating in short messages that evoke strong associations. Also, brands are symbols, and symbols leave room for different interpretations while triggering certain shared associations. Thus brands are applied to bridge different opinions in order to communicate with various actors in a world that has become pluralistic and mediatized.

In this concluding chapter, we wrap things up, outlining the main arguments of the book and contending that interactive forms of branding probably fit well with the conditions of most governance processes, which after all involve multiple actors with diverging values and conflicting preferences about policy solutions. Thus they also tend to have different views about brand values and brands.

8.2 GOVERNANCE AND BRANDING: THE SEARCH FOR CONTENT AND INTERACTIONS

A main story line underlying this book is that we may expect an increase in the use of branding and brands in governance processes. We have already witnessed the beginning of this as the examples in this book show. Put differently, it can be expected that the increase in branding that has taken place in the private sector will also become visible in the public sector. However, branding in governance processes is not the same as branding in the private sector, since governance processes differ significantly from the sale of goods or services. If we analyze how brands can contribute meaningfully to governance processes, we can say that brands are used to manage perceptions, which serves two main functions: firstly, to support the development and implementation of policy solutions in governance processes and, secondly, to create and sustain interactions in governance networks. Thus brand management is a governance strategy that achieves the ends of supporting governance processes and facilitating interactions by starting with perceptions.

Governance: Searching for Solutions

Governance is, among many other things, a search for (new) solutions to societal and administrative problems. Since governance processes are about finding proper solutions for policy problems or realizing service delivery in a situation that is characterized by multi-actor interdependency, actors' goals and ambitions vary or even conflict at the start of governance processes. This means that there is a need for what can be termed goal searching and looking for creative solutions that include and combine actors' different goals and ambitions. Thus one of the key tasks in governance is to develop packages of solutions for policy problems that satisfy the ambitions and interests of various actors. Those solutions must on the one hand address the current problems in the governance network. On the other hand, they must contribute to the development of a coalition of actors that support the solution. After all, in most governance networks the initiator, mostly a governmental actor, is more or less dependent on other actors (public, private, or semi-private) to achieve policy goals or service delivery.

In this book we have argued, on the basis of the marketing and political administration literature, that brands can be applied to facilitate both developing solutions and building coalitions of actors that support those solutions—that is, if branding is applied in a thoughtful manner that is appropriate in the context.

Brands present images, trigger associations, and evoke emotions. The images in branding campaigns can visualize possible solutions and directions for development. In this way, branding can be applied as a strategy for developing ideas and managing perceptions about solutions. The process of developing a brand can be set up in a way that facilitates actors in determining the core values that need to be included and respected in a solution. Also, brands can be used to add particular (emotional) meaning to a solution that motivates actors or softens them up.

In order to be attractive to multiple parties, and motivate the wide variety of actors that is characteristic of many governance processes, the brand needs to be sufficiently tuned to the needs and wants of the actors in the governance process. It is therefore crucial to know the values, ambitions, and interests of the stakeholders and to discuss with them possible brand elements and the values they would like to see incorporated in the brand.

The variety of preferences in governance processes often calls for a brand that is sufficiently broad and open, thus allowing for multiple interpretations. The challenge is to develop a brand that is broad and open but still meaningful to many actors.

Just as in the private sector, brand loyalty in governance processes has to be achieved by satisfying the actor with the brand and the product (the policy measures or the delivered service); but given the uncertainties in governance processes and their political nature, it is more difficult to maintain the support and loyalty of stakeholders without their involvement in the branding process. Stakeholders feel more committed and loyal to a brand if they have been involved in the construction of the brand, because during their involvement they can influence the content of the brand in a way they prefer. Also, they may develop a feeling of ownership regarding the brand. Involving stakeholders in the branding process calls for actively managing the process of brand development and implementation. This conclusion corresponds with the knowledge that governance processes have to be actively managed to be effective.

Governance: Sustaining and Intensifying Interactions

Governance processes are not only about developing content and support but also about interactions between actors. Or one could say it differently: it is crucial to actually build, sustain, and improve the governance network as an interaction network, because these interactions are essential for coordinating actions and organizing collective decision making. When actors are more embedded in the network and their ties become more frequent, this, as research shows, brings with it greater trust (Provan et al. 2009) and better performances (Huang and Provan 2007). This intensifying of interactions and coordination does not happen of its own accord but has to be rigorously managed. Intensive managerial activity, generally called network management, helps to achieve good outcomes in governance networks (see Meier and O'Toole 2007; Klijn, Steijn et al. 2010).

Brands can also contribute to this second element of governance processes. As known from branding in the private sector, brands can enhance the formation of brand communities that are tied together by the brand. The common interest in a brand, and the joint feeling of loyalty to a brand, may cause mutual identification and the strengthening of relationships in governance networks (see Chapter 4). Brands can then function to strengthen the governance network and create a more or less shared identity that acts as a basis for further interaction and collective decision making. Enhancing shared identities and relationships through brands may sometimes have limited direct impact on policy results, but it can facilitate interaction in the network.

Of course the importance of brands in governance processes should not be overstated, even if one succeeds in creating brands that are shared by most of the actors in the governance network. The various actors may share (in the ideal situation!) the brand as a common identity but still retain their own perceptions of policy problems and policy solutions, and have their own interests. This means that at crucial times, when tough decisions have to be made (for instance about costs and benefits), actors may have sharp disagreements despite the shared brand. At such times, the brand may lose its binding function or at least it may not be able to retain that function. In this respect, governance process branding differs from private branding where consumers experience the brand (mostly) individually or in a community where the members are not in competition with each other. Because of these potential conflicts, we will witness more counter branding and challenging of the brand in governance processes than in private branding.

Brands therefore provide opportunities to enhance interactions and decision making in networks, but the effects must not be exaggerated. Actors may ignore the brand, or there may be opposition to the brand. This means again that the creation and use of the brand in governance is generally not something that can be implemented top down without the involvement of the actors in the governance network (unless there is a high degree of consensus in the network). Consequently, it is important that branding is integrated into the interactions and managerial activities in the governance networks. This idea is in line with the various network management strategies that have been emphasized in the literature so far (see e.g. Meier and O' Toole 2007; Klijn, Steijn et al. 2010)

Conclusion: Branding as Part of Interactive Governance

We therefore conclude that, in the context of governance processes, the effectiveness of brands can be increased through interactive development and implementation of brands. This is especially the case if actors may ignore the brand or if there is a risk that actors will oppose the brand if they are not involved in its development.

Developing brands interactively need not be problematic because it is very possible to combine branding activities with network management strategies. Branding and network management can even strengthen each other. The kind of research used in marketing to probe the perception of stakeholders can be used to explore perceptions in networks, as advised in much of the literature about network management; and the construction of the brand can be carried out as a joint action by actors in the network, in which managers deploy strategies to reach convergence in those perceptions. Actually creating the brand may be a vehicle to explore the possibilities of realizing convergence of perceptions in packages of goals and solutions that are acceptable to many actors. The very process of constructing the brand can be used to improve interactions between actors and create a more solid base for collective decision making and trust between them. If properly applied, brands can facilitate joint meaning-making in policy development, and they can become guidelines in implementation processes by representing the guiding core values.

Thus, creating and communicating the brand can be combined with several of the existing managerial strategies to enhance cooperation in governance networks. To incorporate branding in governance networks requires a specific form of branding, which in this book has been labeled as interactive branding (see Chapter 3). It is difficult to combine branding as selling a predefined image and message with the interactive character of governance processes. Particularly in the context of contested governance processes, branding as selling predefined messages may encounter little commitment or support. Stakeholders will not use the brand in their own communication, or they may even try to damage the brand through their communications.

8.3   THE USE OF BRANDS IN GOVERNANCE

It is important, therefore, to integrate branding with the management activities in the governance network; but that does not yet answer the question of when and how we should apply branding in governance processes. Although definite answers are difficult to give because of the significant differences between governance processes, we can determine conditions of governance processes that influence the development and application of brands.

Conditions of Governance Networks That Influence Branding

An important aspect to take into account in governance processes is the degree to which values and perceptions of actors differ or even conflict. Governance networks are characterized by a number of actors who are interdependent because policy solutions or public services cannot be realized without the resources of those actors. On the other hand, however, actors have their own perceptions on the nature of the problem and the optimal solutions, and they choose independent strategies because of that. The consequent complexity and unpredictability of governance processes is enhanced by the fact that decisions are taken in various arenas (Agranoff and McGuire 2003; Koppenjan and Klijn 2004).

If conflicting values are not taken into account in determining the brand values, or if different preferences about solutions are not taken into account in the brand promise, the brand will meet resistance instead of commitment and support. Thus public managers involved in branding need to adjust their branding strategy if the perceptions of the actors in the network diverge or conflict with each other. This presents a paradox. It is probably more urgent to create joint images and a common brand in the case of differing perceptions, but at the same time this is also more difficult to achieve due to varying values, preferred solutions, and webs of associations. In such a situation, creating brands unilaterally will have little effect. It is then elementary to engage in an intensive process between stakeholders to create both sufficient convergence in perceptions and a brand that can satisfy the differences in perceptions. The latter is important because differences in perceptions will remain even if the network manager succeeds in finding common ground and bringing some convergence. Thus it can be expected that when perceptions are more diverse in the network it will be more difficult to "impose" a brand. In such cases, more interactive branding is needed to make branding a success. In cases where there is consensus about policy solutions and the underlying values more instrumental forms of branding can be applied, with less involvement of stakeholders. Another characteristic of governance networks that will influence the possibilities for branding is the interconnectedness of the actors, or, as it is called, the density of the network. It can be expected to be easier to create brands in governance networks characterized by intense interactions between the actors than in networks with low densities. High densities facilitate communications, including communications that are necessary to develop and spread the brand. Also, in such networks there is usually more trust and mutual understanding, which again facilitates the creation of brands. Low density on the other hand will inhibit the communication of the brand. Greater efforts are required to develop a brand community, as the brand managers cannot rely much on the existing connections in the network.

The nature of actors' interdependency will also significantly influence whether and how a brand can be created. Interdependencies between actors can be very different in governance networks. Actors may be tied together very firmly by strong mutual resource dependencies, but dependencies can also be weaker, in which case actors are more loosely coupled. Strong mutual dependencies probably facilitate the process of branding because actors realize that they have to engage in joint sense making and collective decision making, and thus everything that facilitates that will be looked upon more favorably. It can therefore be reasoned that strong interdependencies will have a positive influence on the possibilities of creating and communicating brands. Of course, a distinction could be made here between a core group of actors that is very interdependent and another (large) group of actors that is involved or affected by the governance process but with fewer interdependencies. In that case, the brand could be constructed relatively easily with the interdependent actors, but it could be harder to gain commitment from other actors who do not feel the necessity of developing a common brand.

Further, institutional features of networks may influence branding. Both formal and informal rules may prohibit certain brand features or facilitate them. Informal rules like strong domain demarcations between organizations in the network or strong non-intervention rules may be an obstacle to creating and communicating brands. For example, organizations may prefer to communicate their own brand instead of a (shared) project brand. Also, socially embedded norms may be adverse to branding strategies, for example the norm that branding should be avoided because it is a form of propaganda. The brand manager has to be aware of these institutional features in the branding process.

Tuning Branding to the Situation

Thus to conclude we argue that brands and branding must be tuned to the situation, that is, a specific governance process in a specific governance network. To be able to create effective brands and branding processes, it is important that branding is connected to a network analysis (see Koppenjan and Klijn 2004). A good branding process is connected to a network analysis in which actors' characteristics (perceptions, interdependencies), network characteristics (connections, interactions, institutional features), and characteristics of the decision-making process (strategies, deadlocks, arenas) are analyzed. This provides the brand manager with information on actors' perceptions on problems, the things they find important, and the strengths and weaknesses of the network. This information helps to develop the brand and make it work. It also enables the brand manager or brand initiator to tailor the brand development and communication around the brand to the governance situation in which the actors find themselves.

8.4 LOOKING INTO THE FUTURE

Branding is here to stay, and this holds true not only for the private sector but also for governance in the public sector. More and more public managers view branding as a strategy that fulfills certain functions that are important to them in the context of mediatized and competitive governance processes. The need to communicate in both traditional media (TV and newspapers) and new ones (Internet, Twitter, and so forth) will only increase the demand for visual images that can be communicated swiftly without explaining the whole philosophy behind a policy, service delivery, or project.

A Crowded Brandscape in the Public Sector

However, with an increasing number of brands and the public sector brandscape becoming more crowded, public managers will have to deal more often with brand fatigue among the public. Brand managers will have to find innovative ways of drawing attention to, and communicating the brand. They will have to find ways to make the brand genuinely meaningful to actors; otherwise it will attract only little attention. A more crowded brandscape requires a more continuous and active approach to branding, rather than the one-off approaches that are currently often used. Merely launching a brand by introducing a logo, a slogan, and a set of images will become even less sufficient than it is now. This underscores the relevance of a more interactive approach to branding, because the interactions during the development of the brand help to create a brand that is actually meaningful for the actors in the governance network.

Another way to facilitate brand communication in an increasingly crowded brandscape is through word of mouth. The strength of word of mouth is that the message is communicated to somebody by a known source, and this tends to increase attention and acceptance. People have more trust in what is said about a brand by somebody with whom they have a strong relationship than in what is said by somebody anonymous (cf. Ryua and Hanb 2009). Word of mouth can be applied well through diverse social media, because there people commonly inform each other about what they like. This is also facilitated by social media that have virtual buttons (for example showing a thumbs-up symbol) to easily communicate that one likes something. In the context of governance processes, social media can also be used to monitor communications about the brand. Managers of large projects already follow and analyze Twitter messages and other Internet reactions to policy proposals to get an impression of how their project is being seen by large groups of citizens. Growing attention and the tone of that attention after all can be very important for a project's image. One can expect Internet forums and social media to continue to increase in importance, and this provides new opportunities for communication and branding. However, if branding efforts in Internet communities become too intense or obtrusive, this may harm the community. As explained in Chapter 6, a heavy presence of marketing managers in brand communities may destroy feelings of community (see Heding et al. 2009).

Further Research: Empirical Research on the Effectiveness of Different Branding Strategies

An important question regarding branding in governance processes is whether and how brand communities can develop around public projects, public organizations, or public leaders. Public brands can be used to make places, organizations, or public leaders stand out, and accentuate their uniqueness. Thanks to the accentuated identity, people can relate to the branded object. The question is whether such brands can facilitate the formation of brand communities and strengthen relationships between branded projects or persons and the members of the brand community. It will be interesting to see whether group identities develop, and whether brand communities play a role in the formation of social capital.

To date, there has been hardly any empirical research on branding in governance processes. This is no surprise since in most countries branding in the public sphere has emerged only recently, apart from Anglo-Saxon countries where political branding and place branding have already been in use for some time. A lot of research still has to be done before we fully comprehend what works and what does not work in relation to branding in governance processes. In this book, we have taken a first step in exploring how brands function in governance processes, based on the marketing and public administration literature. We have described mechanisms through which brands influence perceptions, and the processes through which brands can be managed, but the precise effects of various branding activities in different concrete contexts will have to be determined in further empirical research.

Notes

NOTES TO CHAPTER 1

1. See http://www.youtube.com/watch?v=YKUHWD7Yw4s&feature=PlayList &p=796EEE1D767135C2&playnext=1&playnext_from=PL&index=21.
2. This does not mean that the classical political institutions have no position at all. Rather, it indicates that they are mostly part of the governance network and that politics, defined as the authoritative allocation of values (Easton 1965), takes place just as much in the governance network as in political institutions.

NOTES TO CHAPTER 2

1. This view differs from that of authors such as Anholt (2006, 4) who sees a brand as "a product or service or organization, considered in combination with its name, its identity and its reputation." In this view, the product is part of the brand.
2. This description is taken from the American Marketing Association (AMA), which proposed it in the 1960s. It has become a standard for numerous scholars and practitioners.
3. The unconscious process of citizens giving meaning to a place simply by being there, and coupling their identity to the place, can be understood as primary communication (Kavaratzis and Ashworth 2007). Primary communication works directly through particular places, policies, products, or services. Primary communication in the case of cities is about the messages that a landscape or a community radiates. A municipal organization's primary communication refers to the message that the behavior of the organization implicitly communicates. For example, when the organization listens to citizens, this sends out the message that the organization takes citizens seriously. Secondary communication, on the other hand, is about what are traditionally seen as marketing and communication activities, for example advertising, PR, graphic design, slogans, and so forth (see Kavaratzis and Ashworth 2007).
4. This is actually a well-known line in the club anthem of Rotterdam's most prominent football club (Feyenoord). It is often quoted to symbolize the culture of Feyenoord and Rotterdam.
5. During Berlusconi's time as the owner and managing director of several television stations, even before he entered the public sector as a politician, Berlusconi stressed the importance of impression management and radiating positivity and happiness. Berlusconi used to instruct his salesmen "to have the 'sun in their pockets,' to exude optimism and courtesy. They

were forbidden to smoke or have long hair, or beards, or even moustaches" (Ginsborg 2005, 46).
6. Most governance theories take a Cartesian-Comtean perspective, wherein emotion or passion is opposed to reason. Within that perspective, "knowledge is seen as particularly vulnerable to the distorting power of emotions. One of the main purposes of Comte's influential positivist epistemology was to insulate the intellect from the sway of emotions, or 'the sentiments' as he called them" (Wagenaar and Cook 2003, 155). Most branding theories are rooted in the idea that emotions are crucial for making good decisions.

NOTES TO CHAPTER 3

1. Fortuyn was a Dutch populist politician known for his flamboyant style and anti-immigration views. He distanced himself radically from the traditional political parties and their way of conducting politics, critically arguing that their consensualism and technocratic politics covered up existing societal problems around immigration. He argued that the dominant political parties (especially the social democrats) systematically neglected problems experienced by the general public, such as a lack of safety and high percentages of immigrants in many urban communities. Fortuyn became very popular in both his own city, Rotterdam, and the Netherlands as a whole in the year before he was murdered in 2002 by an activist who opposed his views. For more information on Fortuyn and his ideas, see e.g. Fortuyn (1997, 2002), Pels (2003), and Uitermark and Duyvendak (2008).
2. The theory of cognitive dissonance (Festinger 1954) explains that people feel uncomfortable when holding contradictory ideas. People are therefore motivated to reduce dissonance between their ideas, for example by adjusting or denying particular ideas. People may thus deny problems as long as they do not see opportunities to solve them. For governance processes, this means that the development of policy solutions is crucial to the acknowledgment of policy problems.

NOTES TO CHAPTER 4

1. This quote is borrowed from the case study in Michiel Kort's (2011) PhD on URCs and their effectiveness.

NOTES TO CHAPTER 7

1. According to O'Shaughnessy (2001, 1050), *USA Today* in 1996 found that "28 per cent of 188 commercials scrutinized contained questionable usage of technology," such as news conferences that were never held.
2. See e.g. Lees-Marshment (2001) and Reeves et al. (2006) for discussions around the focus on needs and wants of the public (marketing-oriented policymaking). See also Edelman (1988) for a similar critique not directly related to branding.
3. If the meaning of a brand does not change and remains static, brands may wear out soon enough (cf. Tellis 2004). Their effectiveness then diminishes because people grow indifferent to the brand or become tired of it. Especially in political contexts, voters often tire of their branded leaders within a few years.

Bibliography

Agranoff, R., and M. McGuire. 2001. Big questions in public network management research. *Journal of Public Administration Research and Theory* 11 (3): 295–326.
———. 2003. *Collaborative public management: New strategies for local governments*. Washington, DC: Georgetown University Press.
Anholt, S. 2006. *Competitive identity: The new brand management for nations, cities and regions*. Basingstoke: Palgrave Macmillan.
Arnstein, S. R. 1971. Eight rungs on the ladder of citizen participation. In *Citizen participation: Effecting community change*, eds. S. C. Edgar and B. A. Passett, 69–91. New York: Praeger.
Arvidsson, A. 2006. *Brands: Meaning and value in media culture*. London: Routledge.
Bache, I., and M. Flinders. 2004. *Multi-level governance*. Oxford: Oxford University Press.
Balmer, J. M. T. 2006. Corporate brand cultures and communities. In *Brand culture*, eds. J. E. Schroeder and M. Salzer-Mörling, 34–83. London: Routledge.
Batey, M. 2008. *Brand meaning*. London: Routledge.
Baumgartner, F. R., and B. Jones. 2009. *Agendas and instability in American politics*. 2nd ed. Chicago: University of Chicago Press.
BBC. 2008. *ICESAVE savers warned on accounts*. 7 October 2008. http://news.bbc.co.uk/2/hi/7656387.stm. Accessed on 22 March 2011.
Bekkers, V., G. Dijkstra, A. Edwards, and M. Fenger. 2007. *Governance and the democratic deficit: Assessing the democratic legitimacy of governance practices*. Aldershot: Ashgate.
Bennett, R., and S. Savani. 2003. The rebranding of city places: An international comparative investigation. *International Public Management Review* 4 (2): 70–87.
Bennett, W. L. 2009. *News: The politics of illusion*. New York: Pearson Longman.
Benson, J. K. 1982. A framework for policy analysis. In *Interorganizational co-ordination: Theory, research and implementation*, eds. D. Rogers and D. Whetten, 137–76. Ames: Iowa State University Press.
Blichfeldt, B. S. 2005. Unmanageable place brands? *Place Branding* 1 (4): 388–401.
Bol, P., and M. de Langen. 2006. Rotterdam en de Rotterdamwet. *Tijdschrift voor de Volkshuisvesting* 12 (3): 6–11.
Bramwell, B., and L. Rawding. 1996. Tourism marketing images of industrial cities. *Annals of Tourism Research* 23: 201–21.
Braun, E. 2008. *City marketing: Towards an integrated approach*. Rotterdam: Erasmus Research Institute of Management (ERIM).

Braybrooke, D., and C. E. Lindblom. 1963. *A strategy of decision*. New York: The Free Press.

Broudehoux, A. M. 2001. Image making, city marketing and the aesthetization of social inequality in Rio de Janeiro. In *Consuming tradition, manufacturing heritage*, ed. N. Alsayyad, 273–97. London: Routledge.

Brownill, S. 1994. Selling the inner city: Regeneration and place marketing in London's Docklands. In *Place promotion: The use of publicity and marketing to sell towns and regions*, eds. J. R. Gold and S. V. Ward, 133–51. Chichester: Wiley.

CBI. 2007. *Going global; The world of public private partnerships*. Confederation of British Industry. http://www.cbui.org.uk. Accessed on 12 October 2010.

Cobb, R. W., and C. D. Elder. 1983. *Participation in American politics: The dynamics of agenda-building*. 2nd ed. Baltimore: Johns Hopkins University Press.

Cohen, A. 1985. *The symbolic construction of community*. London: Tavistock.

Corner, J., and D. Pels, eds. 2003. *Media and the restyling of politics. Consumerism, celebrity and cynicism*. London: Sage.

Csaba, F. F., and A. Bengtsson. 2006. Rethinking identity in brand management. In *Brand culture*, eds. J. E. Schroeder and M. Salzer-Mörling, 118–35. London: Routledge.

Danesi, M. 2006. *Brands*. London: Routledge.

Davies, N. 2008. *Flat earth news*. London: Chatto and Windus.

De Chernatony, L., and F. Dall'Olmo Riley. 1998. Defining a 'brand': Beyond the literature with experts' interpretations. *Journal of Marketing Management* 14: 417–43.

Delicath, J. W., and K. M. Deluca. 2003. Image events, the public sphere, and argumentative practice: The case of radical environmental groups. *Argumentation* 17 (3): 315–33.

Deloitte. 2006. *Building flexibility: New delivery models for public infrastructure projects*. London: Deloitte & Touche.

De Pers. 2008. Vogelaar geeft sneer naar PvdA. 13 November 2008. http://www.depers.nl/binnenland/261176/Vogelaar-geeft-sneer-naar-PvdA.html. Accessed on 12 October 2010.

Dery, D. 1984. *Problem definition in policy analysis*. Lawrence: University Press of Kansas.

———. 2000. Agenda setting and problem definition. *Policy Studies* 21 (1): 37–47.

Dewulf, A., B. Gray, L. Putnam, R. Lewicki, N. Aarts, R. Bouwen, and C. van Woerkum. 2009. Disentangling approaches to framing in conflict and negotiation research: A meta-paradigmatic perspective. *Human Relations* 62: 155–93.

Driessens, O., K. Raeymaeckers, H. Verstraeten, and S. Vandenbussche. 2010. Personalization according to politicians: A practice theoretical analysis of mediatization. *Communications* 35: 309–26.

Dror, Y. 1968. *Public policy-making reexamined*. Scranton: Chandler.

Dryzek, J. S. 2000. *Deliberate democracy and beyond: Liberals, critics, contestations*. Oxford: Oxford University Press.

Easton, D. 1965. *A systems analysis of political life*. New York: Wiley.

Edelenbos, J. 2000. Process in shape [in Dutch]. PhD diss., Lemma, Utrecht.

———. 2005. Institutional implications of interactive governance: Insights from Dutch practice. *Governance* 18 (1): 111–34.

Edelenbos, J., and E. H. Klijn. 2006. Managing stakeholder involvement in decision making: A comparative analysis of six interactive processes in the Netherlands. *Journal of Public Administration Research and Theory* 16 (3): 417–46.

———. 2007. Trust in complex decision-making networks: A theoretical and empirical exploration. *Administration and Society* 39 (1): 25–50.

Edelenbos, J., E. H. Klijn, and B. Steijn. 2010. Does democratic anchorage matter? An inquiry into the relation between democratic anchorage and outcome of Dutch environmental projects. *American Review of Public Administration* 40 (1): 46–63.

Edelman, M. 1977. *Political language: Words that succeed and policies that fail.* New York: Academic Press.

———. 1988. *Constructing the political spectacle.* Chicago: University of Chicago.

Elchardus, M. 2002. *De dramademocratie.* Tielt: Lannoo.

Elliott, R., and A. Davies. 2006. Symbolic brands and authenticity of identity performance. In *Brand culture*, eds. J. E. Schroeder and M. Salzer-Mörling, 155–68. London: Routledge.

Eshuis, J. 2006. *Kostbaar vertrouwen: een studie naar proceskosten en procesvertrouwen in beleid voor agrarisch natuurbeheer.* Delft: Eburon.

Eshuis, J., and J. Edelenbos. 2009. Branding in urban regeneration. *Journal of Urban Regeneration and Renewal* 2: 272–82.

Evans, G. 2003. Hard-branding the cultural city—From Prado to Prada. *International Journal of Urban and Regional Research* 27 (2): 417–40.

Ewen, S. 1988. *All consuming images: The politics of style in contemporary culture.* New York: Basic Books.

Fairclough, N. 2000. *New Labour, new language.* London: Routledge.

Fenger, M., and V. Bekkers. 2007. The governance concept in public administration. In *Governance and the democratic deficit*, eds. V. Bekkers, G. Dijkstra, A. Edwards, and M. Fenger, 13–34. Aldershot: Ashgate.

Festinger, L. 1954. A theory of social comparison processes. *Human Relations* 7: 117–40.

Fischer, F. 2003. *Reframing public policy: Discursive politics and deliberative practices.* Oxford: Oxford University Press.

Flowerdew, J. 2004. The discursive construction of a world class city. *Discourse & Society* 15: 579–605.

Fortuyn, P. 1997. *Tegen de Islamisering van Onze Cultuur.* Utrecht: Bruna.

Fortuyn, P. 2002. *De Puinhopen van Acht Jaar Paars: Een Genadeloze Analyse van de Collectieve Sector en Aanbevelingen voor een Krachtig Herstelprogramma.* Uithoorn: Karakter.

Fournier, S. 1998. Consumers and their brands: Developing relationship theory in consumer research. *Journal of Consumer Research* 24: 343–47.

Frederickson, H. G. 2005. What happened to public administration? Governance, governance everywhere. In *The Oxford handbook of public management*, eds. E. Ferlie, L. Lynn, and C. Pollitt, 282–304. Oxford: Oxford University Press.

Friend, J. K., J. M. Power, and C. J. L. Yewlett. 1974. *Public planning: The intercorporate dimension.* London: Tavistock.

Gage, R. W., and M. P. Mandell, eds. 1990. *Strategies for managing intergovernmental policies and networks.* New York/London: Praeger.

Gerrits, L. 2008. *The gentle art of coevolution: A complexity theory perspective on decision making over estuaries in Germany, Belgium and the Netherlands.* Published PhD diss. Rotterdam: Erasmus University Rotterdam.

Ginsborg, P. 2005. *Silvio Berlusconi: Television, power and patrimony.* 2nd ed. London: Verso.

Goffman, E. 1986 [1974]. *Frame analysis: An essay on the organization of experience.* Boston: Northeastern University Press.

Gould, M., and H. Skinner. 2007. Branding on ambiguity? Place branding without a national identity: Marketing Northern Ireland as a post-conflict society. *Place Branding and Public Diplomacy* 3 (1): 100–13.

Grainge, P. 2008. *Brand Hollywood. Selling entertainment in a global media age.* London: Routledge.

Greenberg, M . 2008. *Branding New York: How a city in crisis was sold to the world.* New York: Routledge.

Hajer, M. A. 1995. *The politics of environmental discourse: Ecological modernization and the policy process.* Oxford: Oxford University Press.

———. 2009. *Authoritative governance: Policy-making in the age of mediatization.* Oxford: Oxford University Press.

Hajer, M., and H. Wagenaar, eds. 2003. *Deliberative policy analysis: Understanding governance in the network society.* Cambridge: Cambridge University Press.

Hamers, D. 2005. De Øresund: een regio, geen streek. *Ruimte in Debat* 2: 17–19.

Hanf, K. I., and F. W. Scharpf, eds. 1978. *Interorganizational policy making: Limits to coordination and central control.* London: Sage.

Hankinson, G. 2001. Location branding: A study of the branding practices of 12 English cities. *Brand Management* 9 (3): 127–42.

———. 2004. Relational network brands: Towards a conceptual model of place brands. *Journal of Vacation Marketing* 10 (2): 109–21.

Harris, P., and A. Lock. 2001. Establishing the Charles Kennedy brand: A strategy for an election the result of which is a foregone conclusion. *Journal of Marketing Management* 17 (9–10): 943–56.

Hatch, M., and J. Rubin. 2006. The hermeneutics of branding. *Brand Management* 14 (1/2): 40–59.

Heding, T., C. F. Knudtzen, and M. Bjerre. 2009. *Brand management: Research, theory and practice.* London: Routledge.

Held, D. 2006. *Models of democracy.* Cambridge: Polity Press.

Hepp, A., S. Hjarvard, and K. Lundby. 2010. Mediatization—empirical perspectives: An introduction to a special issue. *Communications* 35: 223–28.

Hodge, G., and C. Greve, eds. 2005. *The challenge of public-private partnerships.* Cheltenham: Edward Elgar.

Hofferbert, R. I. 1974. *The study of public policy.* Indianapolis: Bobbs-Merrill.

Holcomb, B. 1994. City make-overs: Marketing the post-industrial city. In *Place promotion: The use of publicity and marketing to sell towns and regions,* eds. J. R. Gold and S. V. Ward, 113–31. Chichester: Wiley.

Holt, D. 2002. Why do brands cause trouble? A dialectical theory of consumer culture and branding. *Journal of Consumer Research* 29: 70–90.

Holt, D. 2004. *How brands become icons: The principles of cultural branding.* Boston: Harvard Business School Press.

Hood, C. 1991. A public management for all seasons? *Public Administration* 69: 3–19.

Hooghe, L., and G. Marks. 2002. *Multi-level governance in European politics.* Lanham: Rowman and Littlefield.

Hoppe, R. 2002. Cultures of public policy problems. *Journal of Comparative Policy Analysis: Research and Practice* 4 (3): 305–26.

———. 2010. *The governance of problems: Puzzling, powering and participation.* Bristol: The Policy Press.

Hospers, G. J. 2006. Borders, bridges and branding: The transformation of the Øresund region into an imagined space. *European Planning Studies* 14: 1015–33.

Huang, K., and K. G. Provan. 2007. Structural embeddedness and organizational social outcomes in a centrally governed mental health service network. *Public Management Review* 9 (2): 169–89.

Iceland Review Online. 2008. *Former Landsbanki owner: Assets will cover Icesave.* 14 November 2008. http://www.icelandreview.com/icelandreview/daily_news/?cat_id=16567&ew_0_a_id=315396. Accessed on 22 March 2011.

Jordan, G. 1990. Sub-governments, policy communities and networks: Refilling the old bottles? *Journal of Theoretical Politics* 2 (3): 319–38.

Kapferer, J. N. 1992. *Strategic brand management: Creating and sustaining brand equity long term.* London: Kogan Page.

Kavaratzis, M. 2008. From city marketing to city branding. An interdisciplinary analysis with reference to Amsterdam, Budapest and Athens. PhD diss., Groningen University.

Kavaratzis, M., and G. J. Ashworth. 2005. City branding: An effective assertion of identity or a transitory marketing trick? *Tijdschrift voor Economische en Sociale Geografie* 96: 506–14.

———. 2007. Partners in coffee shops, canals and commerce: Marketing the city of Amsterdam. *Cities* 24 (1): 16–25.

Keller, K. L. 1999. Managing brands for the long run: Brand reinforcement and revitalization strategies. *California Management Review* 41 (3): 102–24.

Kenniscentrum PPS. 1998. Eindrapport Meer Waarde door Samen Werken [*Final report on added value through cooperation*]. The Hague: Kenniscentrum [*Knowledge Centre*], Ministry of Finance, Projectbureau PPS.

———. 1999. Kenniscentrum Publiek-Private Samenwerking, Voortgangsrapportage PPS [*Knowledge Centre Public–Private Partnership, PPP Progress Report*]. The Hague: Ministry of Finance.

———. 2001. Voortgangsrapportage 2001 [*Progress Report 2001*]. The Hague: Ministry of Finance.

———. 2002. Voortgangsrapportage 2002 [*Progress Report 2002*]. The Hague: Ministry of Finance.

Kettl, D. F. 2000. *The global public management revolution: A report on the transformation of governance.* Washington, DC: Brookings Institution Press.

Kickert, W. J. M., E. H. Klijn, and J. F. M. Koppenjan. 1997. *Managing complex networks: Strategies for the public sector.* London: Sage.

Kingdon, J. W. 1984. *Agendas, alternatives and public policies.* Boston: Little, Brown.

Klapp, O. E. 1986. *Overload and boredom: Essays on the quality of life in the information society.* Westport, CT: Greenwood Press.

Klein, N. 2000. *No logo: Taking aim at the brand bullies.* London: Flamingo.

Klijn, E. H. 2005. Networks and inter-organisational management: Challenging steering, evaluation and the role of public actors in public management. In *The Oxford handbook of public management*, eds. E. Ferlie, L. Lynn, and C. Pollitt, 257–81. Oxford: Oxford University Press.

———. 2008a. *It's the management, stupid! On the importance of management in complex policy issues.* The Hague: Lemma.

———. 2009. Public–private partnerships in the Netherlands: Policy, projects and lessons. *Economic Affairs* 29 (1): 26–32.

Klijn, E. H., J. Edelenbos, and M. Hughes. 2007. Public private partnerships: A two headed reform. A comparison of PPP in England and the Netherlands. In *New public management in Europe: Adaptation and alternatives*, eds. C. Pollitt, S. van Thiel, and V. Homburg, 71–89. Basingstoke: Palgrave Macmillan.

Klijn, E. H., J. Edelenbos, and B. Steijn. 2010. Trust in governance networks: Its implications on outcomes. *Administration and Society* 42 (2): 193–221.

Klijn, E. H., and C. Skelcher. 2007. Democracy and governance networks: Compatible or not? *Public Administration* 85 (3): 587–609.

Klijn, E. H., and I. Snellen. 2009. Complexity theory and public administration: A critical appraisal. In *Managing complex governance systems*, eds. G. R. Teisman, M. W. van Buuren, and L. M. Gerrits, 17–36. London: Routledge.

Klijn, E. H., B. Steijn, and J. Edelenbos. 2010. The impact of network management on outcomes in governance networks. *Public Administration* 88 (4): 1063–82.

Klijn, E. H., and G. R. Teisman. 2003. Institutional and strategic barriers to public–private partnerships: An analysis of Dutch cases. *Public Money and Management* 23 (3): 137–46.

Koller, V. 2009. Brand images: Multimodal metaphor in corporate branding messages. In *Multimodal metaphor*, eds. C. Forceville and E. Urios-Aparisi, 45–71. Berlin: de Gruyter.

Kooiman, J., ed. 1993. *Modern governance*. London: Sage.

———. 2003. *Governing as governance*. London: Sage.

Koppenjan, J., and E. H. Klijn. 2004. *Managing uncertainties in networks: A network approach to problem solving and decision making*. London: Routledge.

Kort, M. 2011. Perspectief op herstructurering; een onderzoek naar het belang van de organisatievorm en managementstijl van de Wijkontwikkelingsmaatschappij. PhD diss., Rotterdam, Erasmus University Rotterdam.

Kort, M., and E. H. Klijn. 2011. Public–private partnerships in urban regeneration projects: Organizational form or managerial capacity? The impact of arm's length, discretionary powers, tightness and network management efforts on URC outcomes. *Public Administration Review*, forthcoming.

Korthagen, I. A., E. H. Klijn, S. van de Walle, and J. Edelenbos. 2011. Complex decision making in mediatized societies: The effects of media attention on network performance. Paper for the International Society of Public Management conference, Dublin, 11–13 April 2011, Panel: Predicting the Performance of Public Networks.

Kotler, P., and G. Armstrong. 2006. *Principles of marketing*. London: Prentice Hall.

Kotler, P., G. Armstrong, J. Saunders, and V. Wong. 1999. *Principles of marketing*, 2nd European ed. London: Prentice Hall.

Kotler, P., and K. L. Keller. 2009. *Marketing management*, 13th ed., Pearson International ed. Upper Saddle River, NJ: Pearson Prentice Hall.

Kotler P., and N. Kotler. 1999. Political marketing: generating effective candidates, campaigns, and causes. In *Handbook of political marketing*, ed. B. Newman, 3–18. Thousand Oaks: Sage.

Kuijpers, G. 1980. *Beginselen van beleidsontwikkeling*. Muiderberg: Coutinho.

Lair, D. J., K. Sullivan, and G. Cheney. 2005. Marketization and the recasting of the professional self: The rhetoric and ethics of personal branding. *Management Communication Quarterly* 18 (3): 307–43.

Lees-Marshment, J. 2001. Marketing the British Conservatives 1997–2001. *Journal of Marketing Management* 17: 929–41.

———. 2004. Mis-marketing the conservatives: The limitations of style over substance. *The Political Quarterly* 75: 392–97.

———. 2009. *Political marketing: Principles and applications*. London: Routledge.

Leeuwis, C., with contributions from Anne van den Ban. 2004. *Communication for rural innovation: Rethinking agricultural extension*. Blackwell: Oxford.

Lewicki, R., B. Gray, and W. M. Elliott, eds. 2003. *Making sense of intractable environment conflicts: Concepts and cases*. Washington, DC: Island Press.

Lindblom, C. E. 1959. The science of muddling through. *Public Administration* 19: 79–88.

Lindblom, C. E., and D. K. Cohen. 1979. *Usable knowledge: Social science and social problem solving*. New Haven: Yale University Press.

Loken, B., R. Ahluwalia, and M. J. Houston. 2010. *Brands and brand management: Contemporary research perspectives*. London: Routledge.

Loken, B., and D. Roedder John. 2010. When do bad things happen to good brands? Understanding internal and external sources of brand dilution. In *Brands and brand management: Contemporary research perspectives*, eds. B. Loken, R. Ahluwalia, and M. J. Houston, 233–70. New York: Routledge.

Lowndes, V., L. Pratchett, and G. Stoker. 2001. Trends in public participation: Part 1—Local government perspectives. *Public Administration* 79 (1): 205–22.

Lundby, K. ed. 2009. *Mediatization: Concept, change, consequences.* New York: Peter Lang.

Luyendijk, J. 2006. *Het zijn net mensen; beelden uit het Midden-Oosten.* Amsterdam: Podium.

Lynn, L. E. (1981) *Managing the public's business, The job of the government executive.* New York: Basic Books.

Mandell, M. P., ed. 2001. *Getting results through collaboration: Networks and network structures for public policy and management.* Westport, CT: Quorum Books.

March, J. G., and J. P. Olsen. 1976. *Ambiguity and choice in organizations.* Bergen: Universitetsforlaget.

Marcus, G. E. 2000. Emotions in politics. *Annual Review of Political Science* 3: 221–50.

Marincioni, F., and F. Appiotti. 2009. The Luon–Turin high-speed rail: The public debate and perception of environmental risk in Susa Valley, Italy. *Environmental Management* 43: 863–75.

Mazzoleni, G., and W. Schulz. 1999. 'Mediatization' of politics: A challenge for democracy? *Political Communication* 16: 247–61.

McAlexander, J. H., J. W. Schouten, and H. F. Koenig. 2002. Building brand community. *Journal of Marketing* 66 (1): 38–54.

McLaverty, P., ed. 2002. *Public participation and innovations in community governance.* Aldershot: Ashgate.

Meier, K. J., and L. J. O'Toole. 2001. Managerial strategies and behavior in networks: A model with evidence from U.S. public education. *Journal of Public Administration and Theory* 3 (11): 271–93.

———. 2007. Modelling public management: Empirical analysis of the management-performance nexus. *Public Administration Review* 9 (4): 503–27.

Milward, H. B., and K. G. Provan. 2000. Governing the hollow state. *Journal of Public Administration Research and Theory* 10: 359–79.

Mirzoeff, N. 1998. *Visual culture reader.* London: Routledge.

Mulford, C. L., and D. L. Rogers. 1982. Definitions and models. In *Inter-organizational coordination: Theory, research, and implementation*, eds. D. L. Rogers and D. A. Whetten, 9–31. Ames: Iowa State University Press.

Muniz, A. M., and T. C. O'Guinn. 2001. Brand community. *Journal of Consumer Research* 27 (4): 412–32.

NAO. 2002. *Managing the relationship to secure a successful partnership in PFI projects.* London: National Audit Office.

———. 2003. *PFI: Construction performance: Report by the controller and audit general* (HC 371 January 2003). London: National Audit Office.

Needham, C. 2005. Brand leaders: Clinton, Blair and the limitations of the permanent campaign. *Political Studies* 53 (2): 343–61.

———. 2006. Brands and political loyalty. *Journal of Brand Management* 13 (3): 178–87.

Negandhi, A. R., ed. 1975. *Interorganisation theory.* Kansas City: Kansas University Press.

Niederkofler, M. 1991. The evolution of strategic alliance: Opportunities for managerial influence. *Journal of Business Venturing* 6: 237–57.

Nienhuis, A. E. 1998. Persuasive communication and communicating persuasion. PhD diss., University of Amsterdam.

Noordergraaf, M., and J. Vermeulen. 2010. Culture in action: The 'Rotterdam Approach' as modernization through tradition. *Public Administration* 88: 513–27.

NRC. 2008. Worstelende Vogelaar te grote last voor PvdA. Last modified on 17 November 2008. http://www.nrc.nl/binnenland/article2060050.ece/Worstelende_minister_Vogelaar_was_te_grote_last_voor_de_PvdA. Accessed on 5 May 2011.

OECD. 2003. *Territorial reviews: Øresund (Denmark/Sweden).* Paris: Organization for Economic Cooperation and Development.

———. 2008. *Public-private partnerships: In pursuit of risk sharing and value for money.* Organization for Economic Cooperation and Development. http://www.oecd.org/document/27/0,3343,en_2649_34119_40757595_1_1_1_3740 5,00.html. Accessed on 12 October 2010.

Osborne, D., and T. Gaebler. 1992. *Reinventing government. How the entrepreneurial spirit is transforming the public sector.* Reading, MA: Addison-Wesley.

Osborne, S. P., ed. 2000. *Public-private partnerships: Theory and practice in international perspective.* London: Routledge.

———. 2006. Editorial: The new public governance. *Public Management Review* 8 (3): 377–87.

O'Shaughnessy, J., and N. J. O'Shaughnessy. 2003. *The marketing power of emotion.* Oxford: Oxford University Press.

O'Shaugnessy, N. 2001. The marketing of political marketing. *European Journal of Marketing* 35: 1047–57.

O'Toole, L. J. 1988. Strategies for intergovernmental management: Implementing programs in interorganizational networks. *Journal of Public Administration* 11 (4): 417–41.

Paddison, R. 1993. City marketing, image reconstruction and urban regeneration. *Urban Studies* 30 (2): 339–50.

Pasotti, E. 2010. *Political branding in cities: The decline of machine politics in Bogota, Naples, and Chicago.* Cambridge: Cambridge University Press.

Patterson, T. E. 2000. Doing well and doing good: How soft news and critical journalism are shrinking the news audience and weakening democracy—and what news outlets can do about it. Paper. The Joan Shorenstein Center, John F. Kennedy School of Government, Harvard University.

Pedersen, S. B. 2004. Place branding: Giving the region of Øresund a competitive edge. *Journal of Urban Technology* 11 (1): 77–95.

Pels, D. 2003. *De geest van Pim: Het gedachtegoed van een politieke dandy.* Amsterdam: Anthos.

Petty, R. E., and J. T. Cacioppo. 1986. The elaboration likelihood model of persuasion. *Advances in Experimental Social Psychology* 19: 123–205.

Pierre, J., ed. 2000. *Debating governance: Authority, steering, and democracy.* Oxford: Oxford University Press.

Pierre, J., and B. G. Peters. 2000. *Governance, politics and the state.* Basingstoke: Macmillan.

Pollitt, C. 2003. Joined-up government: A survey. *Political Studies Review* 1: 34–49.

Provan, K. G., K. Huang, and B. H. Milward. 2009. The evolution of structural embeddedness and organizational social outcomes in a centrally governed health and human service network. *Journal of Public Administration Research and Theory* 19: 873–93.

Quade, E. S. 1975. *Analysis for public decisions.* 1st ed. New York: North-Holland.

Reeves, P., L. de Chernatony, and M. Carrigan. 2006. Building a political brand: Ideology or voter-driven strategy. *Brand Management* 13: 418–28.

Rhodes, R. 1996. The new governance: Governing without government. *Political Studies* 44: 652–67.

———. 1997. *Understanding governance: Policy networks, governance, reflexivity and accountability.* Buckingham: Open University Press.

Richards, B. 2009. The emotional deficit in political communication. In *Emotions: Social science reader*, eds. M. Greco and P. Stenner, 361–67. Abingdon: Routledge.

Rogers, D. L., and D. A. Whetten, eds. 1982. *Interorganizational coordination: Theory, research and implementation*. Ames: Iowa State University Press.

Rose, G. 2001. *Visual methodologies: An introduction to the interpretation of visual materials*. London: Sage.

Rose, N. 1999. *The powers of freedom*. Cambridge: Cambridge University Press.

Ryua, G., and J. K. Hanb. 2009. Word-of-mouth transmission in settings with multiple opinions: The impact of other opinions on WOM likelihood and valence. *Journal of Consumer Psychology* 19: 403–15.

Scharpf, F. W. 1978. Interorganizational policy studies: Issues, concepts and perspectives. In *Interorganizational policy making: Limits to coordination and central control*, eds. K. I. Hanf and F. W. Scharpf, 345–70. London: Sage.

———. 1997. *Games real actors play*. Boulder, CO: Westview Press.

Schön, D. A., and M. Rein. 1994. *Frame reflection: Toward the resolution of intractable policy controversies*. New York: Basic Books.

Schultz, M., M. J. Hatch, and M. H. Larsen, eds. 2000. *The expressive organization: Linking identity, reputation, and the corporate brand*. Oxford: Oxford University Press.

Shama, A. 1976. The marketing of political candidates. *Journal of the Academy of Marketing Science* 4 (4): 764–77.

Shanahan, E., M. McBeth, P. L. Hathaway, and R. J. Arnell. 2008. Conduit or contributor? The role of media in policy change theory. *Policy Science* 41: 115–38.

Smart, B. 2005. *The sport star: Modern sport and the cultural economy of sporting celebrity*. London: Sage.

Smidt-Jensen, S. 2005. Branding and promotion of medium sized cities in the BSR. First interim report produced for the 4th MECIBS Conference, Chojince, Poland, 5–7 June 2004.

Soberman, D. 2005. The complexity of media planning today. *Journal of Brand Management* 12: 420–29.

Sociaal Cultureel Planbureau. 2000. *Sociaal Cultureel Rapport; Nederland in Europa*. 's-Gravenhage: Sociaal Cultureel Planbureau.

———. 2009. Crisis in aantocht? Den Haag: Sociaal en Cultureel Planbureau (oktober 2009)

Sørenson, E., and J. Torfing, eds. 2007. *Theories of democratic network governance*. New York: Palgrave Macmillan.

Steijn, B., E. H. Klijn, and J. Edelenbos. 2011. Public–private partnerships: Added value by organisational form or management? *Public Administration* (forthcoming).

Stenberg, S. 1998. New developments in the Øresund Region. *Scandinavian Review* 86: 33–8.

Stigel, J., and S. Frimann. 2006. City branding—All smoke, no fire? *Nordicom Review* 2: 245–68.

Stille, A. 2006. *The sack of Rome*. New York: Penguin Press.

Stok, J., J. Eshuis, and E. H. Klijn. 2008. Branding kan helpen bij herontwikkeling van wijken. *Tijdschrift voor de Volkshuisvesting* 5: 24–9.

Stoker, G. 1998. Governance as theory. *International Social Science Journal* 50: 17–28.

Stone, D. A. 1989. Causal stories and the formation of policy agendas. *Political Science Quarterly* 104 (20): 281–300.

Strömbäck, J., and F. Esser. 2009. Shaping politics: Mediatization and media interventionism. In *Mediatization: Concept, change, consequences*, ed. K. Lundby, 205–23. New York: Peter Lang.

Sturken, M., and L. Cartwright. 2001. *Practices of looking: An introduction to visual culture*. Oxford: Oxford University Press.

Sunday Times. 2008. An icy blast cuts deep into Iceland. 5 October 2008. http://business.timesonline.co.uk/tol/business/industry_sectors/banking_and_finance/article4881378.ece. Accessed on 22 March 2011.

Susskind, L., and J. Cruikshank. 1987. *Breaking the impasse: Consensual approaches to resolving public disputes.* New York: Basic Books.

Tatenhove, J., B. Arts, and P. Leroy. 2000. *Political Modernization and the Environment.* Dordrecht: Kluver Academic Publishers.

Taylor, M. 2007. The birth and rebirth of the Liberal Democrats. *The Political Quarterly* 78 (1): 21–31.

Teisman, G. R., M. W. van Buuren, and L. M. Gerrits, eds. 2009. *Managing complex governance systems: Dynamics, self-organization and coevolution in public investments.* London: Routledge.

Tellis, G. J. 2004. *Effective advertising: Understanding when, how, and why advertising works.* Thousand Oaks, CA: Sage.

Termeer, C. J. A. M., and J. F. M. Koppenjan. 1997. Managing perceptions in networks. In *Managing complex networks: Strategies for the public sector,* eds. W. J. M. Kickert, E. H. Klijn, and J. F. M. Koppenjan, 79–97. London: Sage.

The Observer. 2008. The party's over for Iceland, the island that tried to buy the world. 5 October 2008. http://www.guardian.co.uk/world/2008/oct/05/iceland.creditcrunch. Accessed on 22 March 2011.

Trouw. 2008. Minister Vogelaar treedt af. 13 November 2008. http://www.trouw.nl/nieuws/article1900655.ece/Minister_Vogelaar_treedt_af.html Accessed on 12 October 2010.

Turner, J. H. 2007. *Human emotions. A sociological theory.* London: Routledge.

Uitermark, J., and J. W. Duyvendak. 2008. Civilising the city: Populism and revanchist urbanism in Rotterdam. *Urban Studies* 45: 1485–503.

van Buuren, A., J. Edelenbos, and E. H. Klijn, 2010. *In woelig Water.* The Hague: Lemma.

van Buuren, M. W., and D. A. Loorbach. 2009. Policy innovation in isolation. Conditions for policy-renewal by transition arenas and pilot projects. *Public Management Review* 11 (3): 375–92.

van Eeten, M. 1999. *Dialogues of the deaf. Defining new agendas for environmental deadlocks.* Delft: Eburon.

van Kemenade, L. 2008. PvdA-top grijpt in; Ella Vogelaar treedt af. *Elsevier.* 13 November 2008. http://www.elsevier.nl/web/10211789/Nieuws/Politiek/PvdA-top-grijpt-in-Ella-Vogelaar-treedt-af.htm. Accessed on 12 October 2010.

van Meegeren, P. 1997. Communicatie en Maatschappelijke Acceptatie: een Onderzoek naar de Houding ten Aanzien van de 'Dure Afvalzak' in Barendrecht. PhD diss., Wageningen University.

van Tatenhove, J., B. Arts, and P. Leroy, eds. 2000. *Political modernisation and the environment: The renewal of environmental policy arrangements.* Dordrecht: Kluwer Academic.

van Twist, M. 2009. *Over (on)macht en (on)behagen in de beleidsadvisering.* The Hague: Lemma.

van Woerkum, C. M. J., and P. van Meegeren. 1999. *Basisboek communicatie en verandering.* Meppel: Boom.

Vavrus, M. D. 2007. The politics of NASCAR dads: Branded media paternity. *Critical Studies in Media Communication* 24 (3): 245–61.

Vogelaar, M. 2010. Een systeem in crises? Een systeembenadering van ontwikkelingen in het Nederlands financieel toezicht ten tijde van crises. Masters diss. Public Administration, Erasmus University Rotterdam.

VROM. 2007. *Actieplan Krachtwijken: Van Aandachtswijk naar Krachtwijk.* The Hague: VROM.

Wagenaar, H., and S. D. N. Cook. 2003. Understanding policy practices: Action, dialectic and deliberation in policy analysis. In *Deliberative policy analysis: Understanding governance in the network society*, eds. M. A. Hajer and H. Wagenaar, 139–71. Cambridge: Cambridge University Press.

Waitt, G. 1999. Playing games with Sydney: Marketing Sydney for the 2000 Olympics. *Urban Studies* 36: 1055–77.

Walsh, K. 1994. Marketing and public sector management. *European Journal of Marketing* 28 (3): 63–71.

Weick, K. E. 1979. *The social psychology of organizing*. New York: Random House.

Weihe, G. 2008. Ordering disorder: On the perplexity of the partnership literature. *The Australian Journal of Public Administration* 67 (4): 430–42.

Weiss, J. A. 1989. The powers of problem definition: The case of government paperwork. *Policy Sciences* 22: 97–121.

Wheeler, A. 2009. *Designing brand identity: An essential guide for the whole branding team*. Hoboken, NJ: Wiley.

Wildavsky, A. 1979. *Speaking truth to power: The art and craft of policy analysis*. Boston: Little, Brown.

Wurman, R. S. 1989. *Information anxiety*. New York: Doubleday Books.

Young, C., M. Diep, and S. Drabble. 2006. Living with difference? The 'cosmopolitan city' and urban reimaging in Manchester, UK. *Urban Studies* 43: 1687–714.

Zajonc, R. B. 1980. Feeling and thinking: Preferences need no inferences. *American Psychologist* 35: 151–75.

Index